ALBERT SLOSMAN

THE ORIGINS TRILOGY
III
AND GOD RESURRECTED IN DENDERA

or primordial theology restored

ALBERT SLOSMAN (1925-1981)

THE ORIGINS TRILOGY III
AND GOD RESURRECTED IN DENDERA

LA TRILOGIE DES ORIGINES III
Et Dieu ressuscita à Denderah
First edition Robert Laffont, Paris, 1980

Translated and published by
OMNIA VERITAS LTD

www.omnia-veritas.com

© Omnia Veritas Limited – 2025

All rights reserved. No part of this publication may be reproduced by any means without the prior permission of the publisher. The intellectual property code prohibits copies or reproductions for collective use. Any representation or reproduction in whole or in part by any means whatsoever, without the consent of the publisher, the author or their successors, is unlawful and constitutes an infringement punishable by articles of the Code of Intellectual Property.

- ... BY WAY OF PROLEGOMENA 11
- ALBERT SLOSMAN 12
- INTRODUCTION 13
- **CHAPTER I** 29
  - THE "CELESTIAL BULL" CYCLE 29
- **CHAPTER II** 49
  - TA NOUT-RA-PTAH 49
  - (The heavenly place) 49
- **CHAPTER III** 63
  - THE RENAISSANCE 63
- **CHAPTER IV** 79
  - THE GOLDEN CIRCLE 79
- **CHAPTER V** 92
  - DIVINE MATHEMATICAL COMBINATIONS 92
- **CHAPTER VI** 108
  - THE FEAR 108
- **CHAPTER VII** 122
  - BALANCING THE EARTH 122
  - (Constellation of Libra) 122
- **CHAPTER VIII** 137
  - THE SKY GODDESS 137
  - (The Constellation of the Virgin) 137
- **CHAPTER IX** 151
  - THE GREAT CATACLYSM 151
  - (The Constellation of Leo) 151
- **CHAPTER X** 166
  - CADET TIME 166
  - (The Constellation of Cancer) 166
- **CHAPTER XI** 180
  - PERPETUAL ANTAGONISM 180
  - (The Gemini Constellation) 180
- **CHAPTER XII** 195
  - THE ADVENT OF ATON 195
  - (The Constellation of Aries) 195

CHAPTER XIII **209**
THE DYNASTIC CHRONOLOGY OF ATH-KA-PTAH 209
ALPHABETICAL INDEX OF HIEROGLYPHIC WORDS 214
NOTE ON THE YEAR 1500 BC 223
OTHER TITLES 227

... BY WAY OF PROLEGOMENA

"Who would not wonder, contemplating the magnitude of this work, how many myriads of men and how many years were needed to accomplish it? The usefulness of this edifice and the well-being it brought to the Egyptian people, thanks to the wisdom of this king, will never be worth recounting.

DIODORUS OF SICILY
(History, Book I, 50 to 52).

"Denderah! This name evokes in all those who have made the classic pilgrimage to Egypt in a felucca on the Nile the first real vision of the purest and most ancient beauty they have ever had of an Egyptian temple!"

G. MASPERO
(Extract from a letter dated 27 June 1900).

"It is time to stop studying information taken at random from a tomb or a temple for its own sake, and to look for the reason for their presence, the relative place they occupy, the link that unites them; in a word, to analyse the thought that went into creating the monuments that contain them.

L. DE ROCHEMONTEIX
(Report to the Ministry de l'Instruction publique, May 1878).

"Who would not fear you, O king of the nations, you of splendour? Among the wise men of all nations and kingdoms, there is none like you!
They have shown themselves to be as unreasonable as they are stupid: all their vain science is just wood!

OLD TESTAMENT
(Jeremiah, X, 7-8.)

Humanity is nothing but a chimera, like furniture unable to recognise its original forest.

A.S.

Albert Slosman

Passionate about ancient Egypt and Atlantis.

Professor of mathematics and expert in computer analysis was involved in NASA's programmes to launch Pioneer to Jupiter and Saturn.

His intention was to rediscover the source of monotheism and write its history.

His search for the origins of everyone and everything led him, by curious and unexpected paths, to fix his attention on the ancient Egyptian civilisation, whose formation and development were approached with an open and independent mind throughout his short life.

Albert was a member of the Resistance during the 2nd World War, was tortured by the Gestapo and later suffered an accident that left him in a coma for 3 years.

Slosman was a person of extremely fragile appearance and health, but animated by an intense inner strength that kept him alive, motivated by the desire to complete a work in 10 volumes that was intended as an immense framework of the permanence of monotheism through time, and which his premature death did not allow him to conclude.

A minor accident, a fractured neck of the femur, following a fall on the premises of the Maison de la Radio in Paris, took his life, perhaps because his body (his human carcass, as he liked to say), already well shaken, could not withstand another assault, however insignificant it may have been.

INTRODUCTION

> *"Solon intended to put the story of Atlantis into verse. He asked about the meaning of the names, and when he learned that the Egyptians had translated the names when they wrote the story, he learned how to translate them into Greek."*
>
> PLATO
> *(Critias.)*

> *"I knew that Athens was a colony of Egypt and that it was there that the Greek philosophers had drawn their knowledge of astronomy. I therefore concluded that it was in Egypt that I should look for the true names of the constellations and their origin with the zodiacal signs."*
>
> CH. DUPUIS
> *(Origin of all cults).*

Throughout the history of the Earth and of all its peoples, each of the great civilising eras has seen the sudden emergence of a human being bearing new ideas that ran counter to those officially professed. And it has subsequently been revealed, either a few years later, or a century or a millennium later, that these ideas were very real and were in fact nothing more than reminiscences of the past.

The example of Galileo is flagrant, who wanted to bring up to date the roundness of the Earth and its movement around the Sun, well known to the ancient Egyptians, and who had to put a gag on his mouth, this actualisation disturbing the Holy Church of the time.

It was certainly to avoid this kind of hazard - or so they thought - that the High Priests who had survived their sunken Mother Country set about recounting their odyssey by engraving it on imperishable stone. Before reaching the land which had become

Egypt, and during a long and terrible Exodus[1], these religious had guided the Survivors towards the Promised Land, without any possible hesitation, towards the land which would become their 'Second Heart'. But the place they had reached was contained in a very wide meander of this blessed wave. These thousands of men, women and children had spent hundreds and hundreds of years crossing the gigantic expanses of sand before arriving, after the Libyan desert, on the plateau that dominated the immense loop of the river in the distance, within which was a verdant oasis that could only have appeared to them as a miracle!

For the High Priests, there was no doubt about the significance of this event: this was where the new "House of Life" should be set up first and foremost, to be the repository of all the Sacred Texts, which had become so difficult to preserve orally in their integrity and in their entirety, due to the sudden deaths of those who had learned one or two chapters as children, but who had not been able to withstand to the end the enormous effort of endurance involved in arriving alive in the Promised Land.

So, long before they could enjoy the fertile land and peaceful surroundings, another prodigious effort was required to re-erect, on this site, what would become the complex of the "Divine-Mathematical-Combinations" and the original Annals of the "Elder-Heart": Ahâ-Men-Ptah, the Amenta, the phonetised nickname of what had so long been the Kingdom of the Ancestors of the Lost Continent. The "Golden Circle" would be scrupulously rebuilt there, to match the one that existed near the observatory at Ath-Mer, the capital of the first sunken part.

The interminable Exodus had taken place over more than eight thousand kilometres starting from the West African coast, where they had been rejected to become "The Survivors". This was the "Setting Place": Ta Mana, so called in hieroglyphic, in honour of

---

[1] For more information, read the first two volumes in *this* series: *The Great Cataclysm*, and *The survivors of Atlantis*, by the same author, published by Ed. Omnia Veritas; www.omnia-veritas.com.

the tens of millions of dead of the Amenta, who lay under the liquid layer of the Ocean by a Sun that had been turned upside down and set there for the very first time, whereas previously it had risen there.[2]

This country, which is Morocco, still bears its ancient Arabic name of "Moghreb-el-Aqsa": the Land of the Sunset. It was the point of departure for the descendants of both Usir and Set, following two routes dotted with rock engravings, some three hundred kilometres apart and roughly following the imaginary line known as the Tropic of Cancer.

The long-awaited and finally found place was initially called Ta Mérit: "Beloved Place", a name that was retained until the first king of the first dynasty unified the entire territory into a "Second Heart-of-God": Ath-Kâ-Ptah, the name that was decided to give it millennia before their arrival by the Survivors of Ahâ-Men-Ptah, the survivors of Atlantis, when they promised to seal the Second Alliance with Ptah in this way. It was this name Ath-Kâ-Ptah that the Greeks phonetised as Ae-Guy-Ptos, a name taken up in French by Egypte.

This unification ceremony took place at a time that had been calculated over a long period of time and preconceived for centuries in terms of its favourable aspects, and was therefore urgently recommended by the Almighty Master of the Universe. It took place at a time when certain beneficial influences were being produced in the heavens, triggered by a very rare 'divine-mathematical combination' that also marked the beginning of a new cycle of God. It was the conjunction of our Sun with the 'Fixed' Sep'ti, which is the Sothis of the Greeks, and more prosaically for us, the star Sirius.

---

[2] In *The Great Cataclysm*, the explanation of the earth's upheaval due to the terrible catastrophe is provided. But it can be found in the chapter of this book devoted to the Denderah zodiac.

A very important fact to remember, and one that has been astronomically demonstrated, is that this exact occultation of Sirius by the Sun only happens once every 1,461 solar years, to the day! This premeditation of the precise date cannot be the result of chance. It was long calculated, meditated on, prepared for and expected; no coincidence can be advanced in such a case, despite the length of time involved!

Indeed, on the very day scheduled for this conjunction, the famous unification of the lands occupied by the two fratricidal clans took place; the triple calendar was reinstituted: the solar calendar, for the popular march of the working day; the sothiac calendar, for the divine counting of the Annals; and the calendar of the Great Year, for the march of time within Eternity.

The daily life of the "Chosen" people began a second time on a first day, that of the month of Thoth - short for Athothis - the son of the first King, who ordered the sacred texts to be rewritten in the language preserved solely for this purpose in all the schools that trained the Scribes.

The calendar once again became a written reality on the 1st Thoth of the 12th year of Sirius in the Annals of Ahâ-Men-Ptah, which became the Platonic Atlantis. That day was July 19, 4241 BC, to write in a mathematical form more easily understood by all readers. This remote date amply demonstrates the intelligence of those who made the calculations: the 'Masters of Measurement and Numbers', the descendants of the ancient Priests who were specially entrusted with the preservation of the Law and its Commandments, in other words, the 'Guardians of the Original Faith', as well as all its Sacred Words.

I know perfectly well that it is difficult to admit such intelligence, combined with a perfect knowledge of the workings of celestial mechanics in such a remote era! I also know perfectly well that it would be very difficult for a contemporary Christian to recognise that monotheism as we know it beyond Jesus, through the Hebrew people, is a much more ancient reality originating in Egypt.

This third volume will explain in detail how the immutable Law of Creation and its Commandments could be reborn on the banks of the Nile in a single moment, since they came from an "Elder Heart" within which lived in peace a "Chosen People", who sadly lost their Eden[3]. So it was at Ta-Nout-Râ-Ptah, the "Place where Queen Nut united the Sun with God", which the Greeks phonetically approximated as "Tentyris" and Egyptologists transformed into "Denderah", that the "Golden Circle" was erected. Four millennia later, all that remained were grandiose ruins, and the Arabs, in their turn, preferred to give it a more colourful name, in keeping what this grandiose site had been. It became "Eerba el Ahanas" or "Mother of the Ruins", which expresses the reality, since Denderah is indeed the first original construction to have taken place in this country.

The "Golden Circle", which took nearly twelve generations of architects to complete, was also inaugurated on the accession of Ath-Kâ-Ptah. From day one, its official name was the "*Double Living House*" of the "*Divine Mathematical Combinations*", adjoining the Temple of the "*Lady of Heaven*". It was therefore placed under the protection of the Great Lady, or the "Virgin Queen": Nut, who first gave birth to her divine son Usir, before giving birth to Usit, whose father was her husband, Geb, the last king of Ahâ-Men-Ptah.[4]

For this reason, all the curious people who later ventured into the immense underground tunnels never saw the light of day again. From legend to myth, it was thus that twenty centuries later, it became a story among the Greeks, who referred to the place as the Great Labyrinth!

But why did the Pontiff of the local College of High Priests originally call it the "Double-House-of-Life", when the sixty-four or so schools adjoining the main temples were simply called

---

[3] The first two volumes provide much greater detail.

[4] Ousir and Ousit became Osiris and Seth respectively in Hellenic phonetics.

"House-of-Life"?... Egyptologists are silent on this subject, having given it no particular importance. However, it is a very important explanation, and one that springs to mind when you understand the purpose of the builders.

The teachers at this school trained only the Priests of your first class, who were destined to become the Master Calculators of the right "Celestial Combinations". In the course of this book, we will see all the gigantic work carried out to this end. But they were intended to provide a live opportunity to study the good aspects of Heaven, in order to promote them so that perfect harmony between Heaven and Earth remained. Masters were trained there, not *one Master*, which would have been a danger if there had only been one school teaching all the astronomical aspects! To avoid a man ending up taking himself for God by influencing his contemporaries and their actions as he pleased. It's easy to understand why there were two schools in the same place, because it was impossible to separate them. One taught the 'Combinations' formed by the aspects of the night sky, represented very accurately to a given scale in a deep underground space; while the other, less buried beneath the earth, drew all the daytime aspects. The Initiates of the second class were the 'Masters of the Day', and their *alter egos*, those of the Night.

Herodotus, in his *History of Egypt*, mentions a large labyrinth with 3,300 chambers, which he locates elsewhere. But there is no doubt that it was the only one of its size ever built in Egypt. A good hundred Greco-Latin authors followed in the footsteps of this writer-historian, if I dare use this metaphor, to speak of numerous Egyptian subterranean labyrinths, built in the shape of tombs in particular, but whose origin in no way predates two millennia before Christ. This did not prevent these writers from unknowingly referring to the first of these: the 'Golden Circle' of the 'Double-House-of-Life' of the 'Divine-Mathematical-Combinations' of the 'Temple of the Lady of Heaven' of 'T-a Nut Ra-Ptah'.

As everything to do with the writing of proper names is subject to caution due to more or less fanciful phonetisations, there are a great many names for the king who ordered the construction of the site of Dendera and who was later known only as the "Great Labyrinth" or the "Mother of Ruins". The most common surnames of this Pharaoh were Osymendias, Mendes and Menes. Of course, refers to a single personality, known in hieroglyphic as Mena.

This name was taken by the first Unifier of the Two Lands in memory of 'Ta Mana', the place where the Survivors landed. In this way, he built a bridge with the 'Sleeping Ones' of Ahâ-Men-Ptah. His name soon became the symbol of the Renaissance of the new generations of Cadets, the very ones responsible for creating the "Second Heart" so dear to the new Alliance between the Creator and his Creatures. Then, from century to millennium, from tales to fantastic stories, Mena became Menes, then Mendes in a transformation whose phonetic secret only the Greeks kept, to become two thousand years later: "Osymendias"!

I have not succeeded in rewriting the true history of Denderah through simple deductions or far-fetched inventions. Not only have I travelled many times to Egypt to verify certain important points, but in the course of my patient research in several French and Egyptian library archives I have been lucky enough to find authentic documents that had been forgotten in dusty cupboards. They contained information of incalculable importance, but which no-one seemed to have taken into account until now. Among them was an unpublished manuscript of almost two hundred pages by a French Jesuit priest, Claude Sicard, who died of the plague in Cairo in 1718. This unpublished book is an alphabetical list of old and new names of ancient places. It also contains a number of accounts of his travels, in which he states, using the Indian ink of the time, that he himself visited all three of the country's labyrinths, but that it was only the last one, located not far from Abydos, that could be described as the "Great Labyrinth". He thus contradicted Strabo the geographer, Pliny, "and so many others who never set foot in Egypt", as he himself wrote.

When you realise that General Bonaparte used the map of Egypt drawn up by Father Sicard before his death to prepare his military campaign on the banks of the Nile, it is easy to understand why I was so interested in this document, the thesis of which will be described in greater detail in these pages.

The story of the famous Denderah planisphere, later known as the Zodiac, transported to Paris in 1822 after an epic journey punctuated by episodes where reality is a thousand times more astonishing than any fiction, will also be scrupulously recounted. From the moment he arrived in Marseille, he was the object of a curiosity rarely seen before or since. Another book will be published on this historic subject, recounting all the ups and downs of this precious monument. All the more so since, when it came to interpreting the "Map of the Sky" engraved on it, the most learned authorities put forward hypotheses and theses that triggered a thunder of vehement protests and partisan dissertations among the most famous Orientalists and archaeologists of the time! The most eminent members of learned and academic societies the world over published 'Letters', 'Criticisms' and other 'Memoirs' consisting of several hundred pages in order to defend their personal point of view, the only one to be right of course, using every trick in the book to demolish their colleagues, good colleagues nonetheless!

Thanks to appended notes, explanations, with the benefit of a century's hindsight on discoveries made since then, will show what remains of all the sticking points concerning what became "The Zodiac". Not forgetting Mgr Affre, Vicar General of Amiens, who became Archbishop of Paris at the same time, and who felt obliged to enter this battle of scholars, by casting anathema on the group who claimed that the monument presented the exact stellar configuration of a sky dating back some twelve thousand years!... This was in 1825, and twelve thousand years ago was not only inconceivable, but perfectly impossible; for let's not forget that in those days, although not too far from us, it was biblical knowledge - and the only valid one - that the father of us all, Adam, was only born in the fifth millennium before Christ, not to mention the fact that the Earth did not yet exist ten centuries earlier!...

Under such conditions, how could apparently sensible people put forward such insane hypotheses, worthy of nothing more than a good excommunication!...

Even Champollion, who dared to write that the first Pharaonic dynasty dated back to 5285 BC, had to withdraw this book from sale "so as not to offend the convictions of pious souls"!

This will help us, strange as it may seem, to better understand the violent physiological upheavals that are currently shaking the whole of Christianity. Its virulent questioning is only the logical continuation of the difficulties suffered by monotheism throughout the most ancient eras. If our priests are questioning the validity of this or that dogma torn to shreds by the Vatican II Council; if believers are doubting their faith in a better future; if religious leaders no longer know how to command to ensure the continuity of the Commandments of the Law, which they perhaps consider too archaic, it is vital to penetrate further into the understanding of the Sacred Texts, and therefore of the 'Hieroglyphics'.

Champollion was responsible for the great popularity of this script. But having had at my disposal, at the same time, almost all the works of the world's Egyptologists, including their 'dictionaries', I could easily see that the solution presented by Champollion just before his death was not only unrealistic, but completely at odds with the foundations of the ancient Sacred Texts.

It is not my intention to open a file on this subject, as a thousand pages would barely suffice! Let's content ourselves with a chronological review of the history of the discoveries made by Champolliones. And we can safely say that it was the imagination of Father Kircher, combined with the erudition of Saint Clement of Alexandria, that gave rise to the fantasies of our French Egyptologist!

Born in the aftermath of the French Revolution, on 23 December 1790, Champollion's youth was far from studious, but he became fascinated with Egyptology when he saw the imprint of the famous Rosetta Stone at the home of his older brother,, a renowned archaeologist in Grenoble. From then on, he embarked on real studies before becoming a pupil of the illustrious Baron Silvestre de Sacy, the Permanent Secretary of the Royal Academy of Inscriptions and Belles-Lettres, who undoubtedly guided the young novice with a master's hand as he took his first steps in his career as an Egyptologist.

So when, a few years after his death, his brother published *Grammaire égyptienne, ou les principes généraux de l'Écriture sacrée égyptienne appliquée à la représentation de la langue parlée*, the work was read with enormous interest and favourable prejudice by many, and with a more critical eye by others, especially as the dedication of the book was made to M. Guizot, Minister of Public Instruction.

The publisher's preface had already raised the eyebrows of some scholars:

It's important to remember that we're talking about the theory of a script, not the grammar of a language.

Which is an understatement, given the title of the book!

Then, still in the same preface, the publisher recalls that "an initial minute had been printed in in-4 format", but that it was subsequently transcribed *in large part* onto a small folio paper that was the subject of the presentation". This was not the least of the ambiguities that startled orientalists of all nationalities when they read it! Nevertheless, in 1831 Champollion was awarded a chair at the Collège Royal as a result of his work. Unfortunately, he died four months later.

From then on, the latent controversy became increasingly heated and partisan. The flagrant evidence of a lack of study of the texts, of observation of the Egyptian monuments, and of a lack of pure and simple logic in the reasoning, was laid bare for all to see. Among the many texts published on this subject, the book by M. Klaproth, a renowned orientalist, literally shattered the varnish of erudition that covered the published work on Champollion's "hieroglyphic grammar".

Klaproth wrote

> *For ten years, people have been talking enthusiastically about the late Mr Champollion's discovery of the phonetic alphabet; but few people seem to have a clear idea either of what it really is or of the results it has produced. But few people seem to have a clear idea either of what it really is, or of the results it produced. And Dr Young is without doubt, in his country of England, the first author of this discovery, since it was in 1818 that he recognised the alphabetic value of most of the hieroglyphic signs composing the names of Ptolemy and Berenice, which correspond with the results obtained ten years later by Champollion!*

And throughout the 175 pages of his work, the author demonstrates the falsity of the arguments of the system advocated, under a title that is both simple and modest: *Observations sur l'alphabet phonétique de monsieur Champollion (Observations on Mr Champollion's phonetic alphabet)*. Methodically, Mr Klaproth asserts observation after observation, adding to them all the differences in transcription noted between the first manuscript and the second edition, proving the flagrant changes that had occurred even in the primitive meanings that had been given to multiple hieroglyphs. And it is highly likely that if the brand new professor at the Royal College had not been prematurely snatched from his young glory, he would have completely revised his position to arrive at a solution far more in keeping with the trouble he had undeniably taken.

For hieroglyphics, after Champollion, continues to be a total enigma for real researchers! Gérard de Nerval summed up the situation and his own perplexity about the period very well:

> *I vowed not to understand hieroglyphics! I started with Sanchoniaton, continued with Father Kircher's Œdipus Aegyptiaca, and ended up with Champollion's grammar after reading the observations of Warbuton and Baron de Pauw. What really disillusioned me about these opinions was a pamphlet by Abbé Affre, who was not yet Archbishop of Paris. After discussing the meaning of the Rosetta inscription, he claimed that the scholars of Europe had agreed on a fictitious explanation of the hieroglyphs in order to obtain chairs of hieroglyphic*

language in all countries, which are usually remunerated with a salary of 6,000 francs[5]!

Having also read the authors cited by Gérard de Nerval myself, I had long understood that if I wanted to understand the meaning of the famous hieroglyphs, I would have to try and find a 'grammar' other than that of our eminent Egyptologist!

In 1834, Archbishop Affre, who appears to be so virulent, wrote a book that caused quite a stir, entitled *Nouvel essai sur les hiéroglyphes égyptiens (New Essay on Egyptian Hieroglyphics)*. A distinguished archaeologist and Orientalist, the Archbishop of Paris wrote this work while he was still vicar general at Amiens, and while the duties incumbent upon him were not in excess of his 'hobby'. It was the following passage that caught the eye of Gérard de Nerval:

> *What a discovery for science if the numerous inscriptions that cover the monuments lining the valleys of the Nile could finally have been explained by another Oedipus capable of penetrating their mysterious symbols! Mr Champollion thought he could realise some of these great hopes. But alas! Mr Klaproth seems to have destroyed this illusion! If anything can demonstrate the impossibility of translating the hieroglyphic inscriptions of Egypt with any success, it is the uselessness of the work attempted for the inscription on the obelisk of Pamphile, and for the Rosetta Stone by following what is written in the "Grammar"! In the case of the former, it has never been possible, following M. Champollion's method, to match the phonetic value of the Coptic words with the meaning of the Greek words, and in the case of the latter, the meaning of the Greek words with the hieroglyphs! If, with the help of a Greek translation, we cannot find the Egyptian meaning of the language spoken under Ptolemy, at the time of the famous Rosetta Stone, what will it be like when, without a translation, we have to interpret the idiom spoken by Sesostris? And M. Champollion has not been able to respond to the request made to him by the illustrious M. de Sacy to publish a special work on both the demotic and hieroglyphic text of the Rosetta monument, even if it is only a study, or even just*

---

[5] *Les Nuits de Ramazan*, by G. de Nerval.

an imperfect draft! It is therefore safe to say that he did not read or understand the second part of the fourteen hieroglyphic lines remaining on the Rosetta Stone!

With full knowledge of the facts, I know what more or less acerbic and furious criticism I will inevitably come up against among the "defenders of the Champollionesque theory" who are still the "Masters of thought" of contemporary Egyptology. I put this part of the sentence in inverted commas, because it is quite clear that eminent personalities who have spent ten years learning this theory, then spent another decade preparing a brilliantly passed doctoral thesis, only to end up teaching for the last twenty years... a sum of nonsense that is all the more enormous because it remains incomprehensible - it is quite clear, I say, that these eminent personalities cannot go down the road of history! The errors are so blatant and so monumental that they in themselves show the ill will of the neurons in their brains, and I hold no grudge against them! Perhaps I would have acted like them if I'd been in their shoes! The roadblock is so clear-cut that you end up wondering, in any case, if it's deliberate.

The site of Dendera, which will be discussed throughout this book, is a clear example of this. As early as 1820, when modern Egyptology began, it became increasingly certain that the great Temple of Isis at Denderah was not only a religious building of the first order, despite its Greco-Roman construction, but also that the latter was a mere reconstruction. This was denied outright by almost all the scholars who researched the site. They even claimed that all the hypotheses put forward about its value and antiquity were pure fabrication! However, not only did two Egyptian Egyptologists uncover the top of the Temple of Cheops on 22 August 1979, just below the western pavement of the present temple, but a number of eminent scholars from the early 19th century, such as Viscount Emmanuel de Rougé in France and Mr Dümichen in Germany, called for a proper understanding of Denderah. The first Egyptologist, in a remarkable work on the monuments of the first six dynasties, often refers to those of the curious site of this single loop of the Nile.

In particular, M. de Rougé mentions an inscription found in one of the many subterranean passages that run beneath the great temple, and which refers to a very ancient papyrus found in a wall of the ancient building erected on the orders of Pépi-RaMéri, which relates the construction of the first temple of the Lady of Heaven (Isis) according to the plans of the Followers of Horus, drawn on gazelle skins and carefully preserved. Knowing that the "Followers of Horus" were the predynastic kings of the earliest times, this is a historical way of recognising the origin of Denderah and its astronomical site as being much earlier than Menes himself. And this will be proved in the chapters that follow.

Numerous other documents confirm this anteriority. In particular, a papyrus preserved in the Cairo Museum, signed by the Royal Scribe of His Majesty Khufu (the famous Pharaoh Cheops, which is the Greek phonetisation). It relates that it was on the orders of his king that the temple of the goddess Isis was rebuilt for the third time, following carefully preserved earlier plans.

As for the notoriety of the site itself, it is the subject of numerous documents, and it seems that here again, an improbable imbroglio later turned it into what became known as the "Great Labyrinth"! Most of the time located in the Nile delta, and impossible to find for this reason, it was an unpublished document by Father Sicard, who died in Egypt in 1718, that enabled it to be located at Denderah, and to be substituted for the "Golden Circle", a gigantic construction with 3,240 rooms, from which only fully-fledged initiates could find their way out!

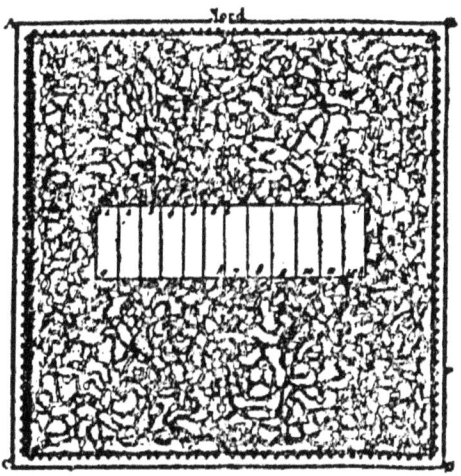

A labyrinth imagined by Herodotus and the geographer Strabo, which has nothing in common with the labyrinth of Denderah, but which bears witness to its complexity.

Ancient texts attest to the sanctity of the site. One of them was found in Tanis, the ancient capital at the other end of Egypt, and comes from the first king to live there: Mêri-Râ. Here is the text, written in high script, and its translation by Viscount Emmanuel de Rougé, which I won't change because this is no place for polemics:

"The king of Upper and Lower Egypt, Meri-Ra, lord of the house of the double diadem, he who loves (his race?), the triple victorious Horus, Pepi, son of Hator, mistress of Denderah, endowed with all life.

What is certain in this text from the Fifth Dynasty is that the name Denderah is there as the name of a temple, and that that of Hator, "the mother of Horus", and therefore of Isis, is attached to it.

This was formally recognised by M. de Rougé, albeit in legendary form, as he explains in a note concerning this hieroglyphic text.

This title occurs several times in the legends of Mêrira-Pépi. The explanation has been given to us by M. Dümichen's recent publication on the underground passages of Denderah. We now know that Pepi had worked on the Temple of Hator, which, according to legend, had existed at Dendera from the earliest times.

It is certain that all these nineteenth-century Egyptologists came up against the Church's lack of understanding of the very great antiquity of the buildings of ancient Egypt. Fortunately, times have changed since then, and all researchers are trying to re-establish the true chronology of the first chapters of the Old Testament. But we may still find ourselves in a period of intellectual stalemate such as the Elders experienced. Their conception of the divinity and its Creation, which was revealed to them, should have ensured them a popular perenniality on the banks of the Nile, which, as the Celestial River on earth, guaranteed them harmony with Heaven. Yet they have completely disappeared as beings made of flesh! And this only stems from the most serious flaw in reasoning that cannot be forgiven!... And we are currently at the same critical point where Good is tipping over into Evil, and nobody can understand why or how. *Because it seems absolutely impossible for human reason to reason in any other way than the narrow path of automated reasoning, where the very concept of God has become unreasonable. Humanity is no more than a chimera, like furniture that is incapable of recognising its original forest!*

Chapter I

THE "CELESTIAL BULL" CYCLE

> "His *mother Nut stretches out her hands towards him in greeting, saying:*
> *- The Imperishables adore you and call upon you:*
> *"Hail to you, O Celestial Bull!*
> *You rise from the ocean of heaven to come to the aid of your cadets.*
> A. Scharff
> *(Aegyptische Sonnenlieder)*

> "O *you celestial ladies, rejoice! He has returned to heaven, among you, his sisters. He speaks like thunder, shaking the Earth with fear, for it is he, Osiris!*
> *And he raises his voice against the ungodly*".
> Pyramid Texts
> *(Line 349 ff.)*

The most physically painful historical episode in the annals of the survivors of Ahâ-Men-Ptah was undoubtedly the interminable flight into the desert, in pursuit of a land that seemed inaccessible. In fact, it did not appear to them until around four hundred years before the Sun entered the constellation that had taken the name of Taurus in honour of Osiris.

Those who had left the Land of the Sunset three millennia earlier had undoubtedly done so only to obey their Priests, who had constantly foretold them that, in exchange for a new way of life, they would find another place that would be blessed by God. For the atonement could not end at sunset, where millions of their ancestors lay asleep in their Mother Country, on the continent that had been their 'First Heart', and which the wrath of Ptah, the one God who created all things, had wiped from the face of his creation: the Earth.

Of these Elders, there was absolutely no tangible trace left among the survivors of the cataclysm, apart from the indisputable fact that they were the Cadets: the great-grandchildren! Everything had been lost in the turmoil, except hope.

For them, who had wandered so much and more, where were reality, fiction, utopia, legend and above all nightmarish fabrication? They knew the Past only through the oral reports that the priests distilled for them every morning that God made after the prayer at sunrise. And the words of the orators remained engraved deep inside them. As, moreover, courses designed to perpetuate Knowledge were compulsory, future generations were assured of not losing any of these precious memorised archives.

The depths of their fatigue had been exceeded long ago, and the implacable, torrid Sun was still burning the skins of all human creatures! And their supreme support during this long and exhausting march had been that of the Elder: the Pêr-Ahâ, whose hieroglyphic name was much later phonetised by the Greeks as Pharaoh. With perfect knowledge of the past and the future, he had lavished his divine encouragement on them day after day. He had been strongly supported in this task by the Priests, the Servants of God, who, as infallible guides, had always found the right path despite the burning sand that always seemed the same with every step taken, and which never seemed to want to end!

Other difficulties had constantly delayed the cohort's progress. Periodically, it was attacked by the hordes of the "Set Rebels". Any stragglers were massacred and the women abducted!

For a second multitude was advancing at a forced march along another, higher parallel line, towards the same geographical point. They were convinced that there was a magnificent land beyond this sea of sand, and they absolutely had to take control of it before the Followers of Horus seized it for their exclusive profit. This was, of course, the narrow-minded and vindictive view of those who had caused both an original catastrophe and a family split.

At least, that was the opinion of the Servants of God, who despised the Sun worshippers. This did not, however, prevent certain older members from being saddened by this fratricidal war, which no longer meant anything after so many centuries of misery and suffering. For Set and Osiris, the father of Horus, had both been born of the same mother: Nut.

For the Priests who led the two clans under banners so different because they personified Good and Evil, the way of thinking pushed towards domination of one by the other. While those of the Eldest of God were not overly concerned about their success, since the predestined times were coming, and then nothing could be changed about what was written in the "DivineMathematicalCombinations", the same could not be said of those of Set who, while interpreting the signs from heaven differently, were trying by force to supplant their brothers before the fateful date set, when any change in events would be forbidden to them!

This final day was the same for both opposing camps: 24 May 4608 BC[6]. At the very moment when the Sun, following its retrograde course, entered the influence of the constellation of Taurus, all attempts by Sun worshippers to dominate would be over, because Osiris had become the Celestial Taurus, master of Measure and Number, the one who would be able to direct his beneficial influences solely towards the Cadets descended from Horus, his elder, and not those of Set the hated because of his murderous deed!

And 23 May, the day before the memorable day, marked the end of all the interminable battles that had bloodied the two offspring for so long. The outcome of this last battle had remained uncertain until nightfall, such had been the ferocity of the fighting. Success had not been achieved simply by arms, the Followers of Horus

---

[6] Throughout this book, we will adopt the current dating system, which requires no explanatory notes, since the months and years on the banks of the Nile are different.

being no stronger than the descendants of Set, but by a kind of mental fluid that had sent a psychic wave through the opposing camp. Everyone was aware of the advent of the Celestial Bull the following day, and the cries of the soldiers of Osiris far exceeded the power of those who claimed to be of the Sun.

Faith in the Bull's inevitable final and complete victory had overcome the deceit and savagery of fratricide. And the surrender took place in the early hours of 24 May: that of a troop that was still very valiant, but which had nevertheless bent its knees in submission to the only Master of all: the Pêr-Ahâ *Men-Nar-Mer*, or 'the Beloved who comes from the Sunset'.

The predictions of the ancient prophecies, repeated by the successive Guides who had brought the Survivors here, had not lied! The Divine-Mathematical Combinations, the geometrical convolutions designed by God in His Creation, which described the celestial configurations of good and bad, could well have predetermined the future. In any case, they were used to predict the future and to foresee possible responses.

That's what was done for that primordial day of 2 May 4608 BC.

To explain this dating astronomically today, there are no grand algebraic formulations to write down, but simple numerical applications to figure out according to meticulous celestial observations. Nowadays, this description would be called the "Precession of the Equinoxes". This phenomenon is based on the difference, in the human eye's field of vision, in the position of the Sun at a fixed point 0. Although imperceptible each year, this difference takes on considerable importance over the years.

In one year, the retreat from the 0 point will be 50 seconds and $2/10^e$ of an arc in space. In general, 0 is the spring equinox, i.e. the point where the Sun enters the constellation Aries, on 20 March.

In 72 years, the Sun will have retrograded by just one degree. This means that in 2,160 solar revolutions, a constellation will have been crossed, and that if nothing disrupts the navigation of our star of the day, in 25,920 years it will have completed one complete revolution on itself, or 360 degrees.

It is therefore relatively easy to calculate the position of the Sun on a given day, whether it is in the future or in the very distant past, because we always know its position as it moves backwards by easily following its entry through the constellation that precedes, rather than follows, it. It is for this reason that the Denderah Planisphere's map of the heavens is accurately dated to 9792 BC, the year of the Great Cataclysm that engulfed Platonic Atlantis. Next came the constellation of the Scarab, which then took the name of Crab, then Cancer; this was followed by the constellation of the Two Brothers, which became the Twins, then Gemini, before arriving at Taurus, which has always had this name since the death of Osiris.

And the Sun's retrograde entry into this part of the sky had long been scheduled for 24 May.

According to the Prophets and Priests who later spoke on their behalf, the Sun was leaving its place of evil in a configuration led by two brilliantly bright "Fixes", but whose non-complementary colours never ceased to clash. This period of 1,872 years had also been punctuated, during the Sahara crossing, by exhausting and bloody battles, precisely between two almost twin brothers: Ousir and Ousit, which in Greek became Osiris and Set.

The Prophets had assured us - but was it they, or the young Priests? -that if there was no global agreement on the day Ra, the Sun, entered the abode of the one who had become the Celestial Bull, Ptah, the eternal God, creator of all things, would be angry with an anger even more terrible than that which had triggered the end of their First Heart. The first day of this glorification of the Son necessarily had to begin with Peace on Earth as it would be in Heaven thanks to Osiris.

Viscerally frightened by the obstinacy of the Followers of Horus in defending themselves, and by the determination they had shown in crossing the immense desert, Set's descendants realised on 23 May that they would get nowhere, and that it was better to give in *for the time being at least!* For this was the only way to keep the survivors of the two populations intact on the same land that was to become Ath-Kâ-Ptah, phonetised as Aegyptos in Greek and Egypt in French. This hieroglyphic name means: Second Heart of God. Which is understandable, since that of the Motherland was the Elder Heart of God: Ahâ-Men-Ptah.

That's why this fratricidal struggle came to an end at dawn on 24 May, just as the Sun was rising in Taurus for a period of 2,304 years[7]. And to make this event a reality, a Pêr-Ahâ became master of the two clans, with the mission of organising the 'Heart' in the best interests of all. This, from the land of the Blessed Sleeping Ones, must have calmed the immense torments of the great Queen Nut, the last divine mother to give birth in the "First Heart" to both a Son of God and a Son of the Earth, making them the worst enemies who would continue their hatred, generation after generation, right up to this day of 24 May.

It was from this memorable date onwards that the good Lady Nut, regardless of the theological ideas of each group, became the "Good Lady of Heaven", the "Goddess, the Protector of the Cadets", and a thousand other beneficial names that reminded everyone that she was the original Mother of the two multitudes.

What's more, the sacred language, which took the Hellenic name of Hieroglyphic, perpetuated its silhouette and its spirit, making it the bridge linking the "Two Earths", the Western one engulfed at sunset, and the Eastern one that had allowed the rebirth of the survivors. Stylized, this figuration became the new sky

---

[7] The length of the constellations is not 30° as in the zodiacal signs. It follows that the equinoctial duration is not the same for all of them. They are calculated as follows at Denderah: Leo and Virgo, 2,592 years each; Cancer and Gemini, 1,872 years each; Taurus and Aries, 2,304 years each; Pisces and Aquarius, 2,016 years each; Capricorn and Sagittarius, 2,448 years each; and Scorpio and Libra, 1,728 years each. That's 25,920 years for 360°.

inverted since the cataclysm. This is how it appears in the engraving below, which is certainly Ptolemaic imagery, but it is significant.

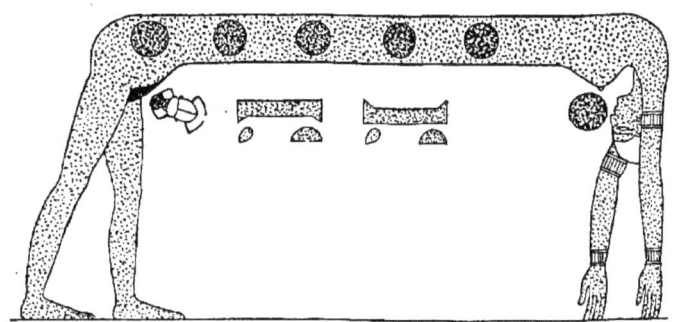

Beneath the body of the sky goddess is the same presentation, stylised in hieroglyphic form. In 1, it's the sky as it is today; in 2, it's the sky as it was before the Great Cataclysm.

The Good Lady Nut undoubtedly had to use all her influence to consolidate the very precarious agreement established on this first day of the cycle of the Celestial Taurus. The second homeland, this 'SecondHeart', was still only a promised place: Ta Merit, until the new covenant with God was promulgated in the time allotted for that purpose. And although this beloved place was graced with all the blessings bestowed by Hapy, the Great River, it nonetheless remained under the exclusive dependence of Ptah.

The act of allegiance to the Pêr-Ahâ *Men-Nar-Mer, a* direct descendant of the Elder of God, Osiris, was solemnly read and sealed by the priests before the chiefs of the two clans, including *Ra-Seti, the invincible Double of Set,* leader of the Rebels.

This unification of the descendants of the Two Brothers living on a single territory took place according to the ritual instituted millennia before for this planned submission. This is why it is known in its entirety. The Annals have preciously preserved it among the traditional texts of the Book of the Four Times of Denderah. Now well known, it is often quoted under the title: *The two Masters said.*

There can be no doubt that, above all, it was an oath of allegiance to the almighty God, who alone could impose on all a law against which the strongest of men could do nothing! This profession of faith took place on the banks of the great river, on the very spot where the first pioneers of the long cohort of survivors arrived, at the very bottom of the loop of the western bank of the Nile, where there was an Edenic oasis!

This place immediately found its own name, to thank God (Ptah), the Sun (Ra) and their mother Nut: Ta-Nout- Ra-Ptah. For four millennia, it continued to bear this blessed name, three times blessed and protected. Then it became phonetically in Greek: Tentyris, before becoming in Arabic: Tentira and Dendra, and finally in French: Dendérah.

But in those days, so long ago that it makes you dizzy to think where your ancestors were at the same time, there was still nothing but a desire for union and unification. For nearly three hours, the two religious leaders, the "An-Nou", had shouted each sentence of the oath loudly to be heard by all, their eyes raised towards God and the Sun, while the crowd of faithful from both clans chanted in chorus, hands raised in imploration of the celestial blessing.

Here is the conclusion of this long text, engraved many monuments dating back to the ancient empire, and subsequently repeated in other forms:

"The Two Masters swore to the Great River: - *Your celestial springs will be the springs of our lives, for they will ensure every resurrection of our lives.*"

"They swore to the people gathered together: -*From now on, you will live in accordance with the Commandments of the Law of the Lord, for it is these that will make your life possible on Earth and afterwards in Heaven. You will nourish the soil with your work. And the soil, in turn, will feed you with its grain and its fruit.*

"They swore to the assembled chiefs of the Uhu[8] of the Two Lands

— *Your authority will remain in the image of your emblems, for as you rule in your provinces, so will your people live.*"

Finally, they swore, raising their arms to heaven, in the face of Ptah: "O *you, Lord of Eternity, Ptah the Almighty, let your Law and its Commandments be, from this day forward, our sole Guide and our only concern, so that our daily actions are not tainted in any way during our earthly navigation. Our descendants will thus be able to conform to your celestial harmony, without the fear of a Great Cataclysm! May the Wisdom, written for us by the unfolding of the Divine Combinations, penetrate each one of us, inspire us and help us to keep our Faith in You on earth, and to prevent us from committing Evil. We will then be able to live again eternally in the Blessed Kingdom of the Redeemed. For there is only one God in Heaven and on Earth: Ptah!*

The whole assembly, grouped together in the natural cirque stretching to the river bank, repeated the name of Ptah three times in a joyous clamour that reverberated in a sonorous echo against the cliffs. The ceremony was over, and a great weight seemed to have been lifted from all the chests of the former enemies. But how many really believed that all the infighting was over? And yet, in reality, understanding and unification had become a reality on 24 May, the first day of the cycle of the Celestial Bull!

The prestige of the priests of Ptah was strengthened thanks to the prophecies of their predecessors, which had been fully fulfilled. From now on, the territorial administration had to be organised in accordance with divine instructions, so that the peace so dearly won would last forever. And the Pontiff, An-Nu, realised that to achieve this, his years were sadly numbered. The construction of the monument to the glory of Ptah had to be speeded up, so that everyone could thank the Creator for his blessings. The 'Golden Circle' complex at Ath-Mer, the ancient capital, also needed to be

---

[8] Uhu is the Greek name, or the French province.

rebuilt as quickly as possible in this ideally located site. The scale of the architectural plans, which were now piling up at an impressive rate, frightened those responsible for teaching the new generations. But with a shrug of his shoulders, the Archpriest dismissed this minor objection, since the Double School devoted to the study of Divine Mathematical Combinations would depend solely on the Masters of Measurement and Number. For on this Knowledge of auspicious and inauspicious astral configurations would depend the people's proper obedience to God's Law.

The High Priest, head of all the clerics on both sides from that day on, *Bâ-En-Pou,* 211[e] a direct descendant of Anepou, could only be satisfied with the way the hours had gone. But he had to be ready for the future that was about to begin.

And as we continue the story of the survivors of the Atlantis Survivors, the Pontiff took the few steps separating him from Pêr-Ahâ, before whom he bowed deeply. The Elder made no secret of his joy at this union, which placed the two clans under a single sceptre: his own.

But the An-Nu, having no desire to show too much public submission to the king, moved away from the improvised throne, as well as from the shore, where the beneficent wave provided some coolness. He was followed by the Keeper of Traditions, a priest of the first class, and the only living Horoscope, who was, as his name implied, the Keeper of the Hours. Clad in the priestly purple, the highest honour bestowed on this initiated priest, he supervised with an impassive face the preparations for the work of the Golden Circle, while diligently watching over *Bâ-En-Pou,* his only leader after Ptah. Between them, the three of them formed such an unshakeable traditional block that they had withstood all the blows of the leaders of the Sun-worshipping sect.

The Pontiff, as he walked with measured steps and welcomed the tributes of the crowd united in a single acclamation, thought about the distance he had travelled and his complete victory. He felt too old to change his opinion, and he had remained rather dry with regard to the priests of Ra. But how could he suddenly forget the past millennia during which wars, massacres of innocents and blasphemous sacrileges had been their daily lot? And the big question that still gripped his chest was whether they would live as brothers for much longer! All that remained was to hope that in this cycle dedicated to his son, Ptah would make ample use of his kindness to make up for the differences that would inevitably arise, and iron out the difficulties.

How many murderers could there be in the long line of yellow robes of those of the Sun whom he was passing at the moment and who were greeting him respectfully?... The Pontiff preferred not to dwell on this distressing question. However, the students from the two religious colleges were mixed together and were giving him the same sign of veneration as he passed.

Still filled with a sense of pride at the success of the day's premeditated plan, the AnNu stopped walking for a few moments to allow the two following him to catch up. The three clerics resumed their progress at the same slow pace, seeming to measure it by competing with the length of time, second by second.

In particular, the Pontiff wanted to talk to his "trusted men" about the secret arrangements for drilling the foundations of the gigantic underground tunnels planned to lead into the Double House of Life. The joyous shouts around them created a barrier to this private conversation. The path they followed, and from which everyone respectfully stepped aside, was made of fine red earth that had already been well compacted, and led to the temporary building, still made of mud bricks using the primitive method. It was used to teach neophytes, the future priests of the fourth class, the beginners. There were still more than three centuries to go before the passage of time was restored, and there was now every opportunity to complete the Great Work that was the Golden Circle with its Double Study by day and by night.

The Year of God, which decided the calendar, would not begin until 4244[9]. And it was only from this time onwards that the "Masters of Measurement and Number" would be initiated. Until then, apart from the Pontiff, no one would have access to complete Knowledge. It was for this reason that supreme power would belong not to a single class of priests, but to two, so that none of them would claim to be a god one day!

Hence this huge building, planned down to the last detail and divided into two distinct parts within the same school.

As the road climbed, the Pontiff lengthened his stride slightly, straightening his waist so as not to slow his companions' pace any further. His old body was cracking under the strain of the last few years. It was undoubtedly coming to the end of its earthly usefulness! As it was absolutely necessary not only for it to last, but also for him not to let his physical suffering show, he forced himself to smile to satisfy the eyes of his two companions, who were constantly watching him furtively with concern.

Bâ-En-Pou spoke in a good-natured tone, to the older of the two, who was so full of his role as Keeper of the Hours:

- Everything seems to be ready for the major works to begin, my good Tan-Pet; is the same true of your solar calculations?

- Ra is not only resplendent on his dazzling golden boat, but his navigation is so precise, thanks to Ptah, that calculations are simplified. My merit in dating this mathematics is slight, O venerated Pontiff!

---

[9] This is the year determined by Sirius, whose revolution is equal to 1,461 solar years. Year 1 begins with the conjunction of the Sun and Sirius. Since the last conjunction took place in the year 1322, the year the Pontiff is thinking of is 4244 BC, well over three centuries later than the one we are dealing with here.

The pontiff gave a brief smile of satisfied connivance at this onslaught of modesty:

- Don't underestimate your knowledge, Tan-Pet, especially when the results are so important. To tell you the truth, I'm a bit worried about the start of this work!

- You are wrong to be, O Pontiff.

- I know, but age is blurring my vision a bit! Ptah, in all his mighty goodness, ensures that Ra's light does not fall any faster, or any less brightly on any inhabitant of this second earth. Whatever the Creator's wrath, he will shine the same light throughout the duration of Usir's blessing upon us. The presence of the Son, the Celestial Bull, at the zenith of the azure for more than two millennia should not put us to sleep with this prophecy.

Horoscope grimaced quickly at the Pontiff's pessimistic tone, and preferred to remain silent. It was the other, younger priest who replied:

- Are you afraid, O Venerable One, that the sacred work we have to do is beyond our capabilities?

- Fear? That word in your lyrics shocks me, Rabou-Nit!

- Yet faced with the immensity of the task before us, O venerable one, I feel very apprehensive.

The Patriarch suppressed a grimace of pain at a sharp sting in his right side, and nodded:

- You know better than anyone, you who have been the Guardian of our oral traditions since our annals drew the word 'End' with the blood of our Ancestors, that the word fear can no longer have any meaning since the horrible cataclysm that wiped out our First Heart.

Horoscope took the opportunity to point out:

- Nevertheless, the reintroduction of Knowledge among human beings can be frightening! We've fought so hard to achieve peace, and now we're sowing the seeds of a gangrene that could rot everything in a cataclysmic reproduction in a few centuries or millennia!

The Pontiff pouted bitterly:

- A similar conversation certainly took place a long time ago. This Knowledge was on its way to perdition, just as it is today. But it was not up to God's supreme servant to decide whether or not future generations should receive this heritage from Osiris. It's a burning issue, with the potential to reduce not just humans, but the whole Earth, to ashes!

- Are you thinking, O Pontiff, that Knowledge is the Sacred Fire?

- Fire warms, Rabou-Nit; it is fertile and life-giving like Knowledge... when it is kindled by a Wise Man! Now, before the end of our Heart, those who, for personal reasons, lit a fire using Knowledge, without even suspecting that they were not magicians or prophets, but unfortunate sorcerer's apprentices, could not extinguish that Fire! All their lives were destroyed, and they were engulfed in the flames of the Past to prevent the Future from coming into being. Despite this unforgettable catastrophe, the Pontiff of the time decided to safeguard Knowledge because there were Survivors. And that's how I see it now, even if a more horrible cataclysm befalls our people four or five millennia from now!

The three of them lost themselves in thought for a moment, oblivious to the jubilation around them at the beneficial prospect of this Celestial Taurus cycle, which was opening today under such auspicious conditions.

The Pontiff, who was contemplating them, admitted to himself that this very vulnerable multitude would not hesitate to launch into new heresies if they were not kept firmly chained by intangible dogmatic rites at all times!... And the very old man shook himself and sighed. Man was made in such a way that he would one day forget the past and its dramas. But for the moment, he had better things to do. So he again:

- I have no advantage over you, Habut-Nit, other than the totality of Knowledge and being its sole possessor. However, it is in danger of becoming perishable through the fault of my flesh, which must not happen. This teaching that I swore, decades ago, to preserve in its integrity in order to pass it on, must now be learned in its entirety by someone else. This is why the building of the Golden Circle cannot be delayed by a day, as my days are numbered!

- Our architects are waiting for your orders to have the workmen dig through the friable earth to reach the rock. Soundings indicate that the sand accumulated by the winds reaches a height of eighteen cubits[10], which is a good quantity for our undertaking.

- I will give the order tomorrow, at sunrise and after the morning blessing. I am not eternal, and it is only time for me to finish transcribing the various formulas buried deep in my memory so that they are not lost either.

- There's no hurry, O venerated Pontiff!

- Yes, I'm under no illusions about what's left to me. But I've had to redo the drawings of the astral configurations. I had reproduced them on tablets that were too crude, made from a macerated decoction of palm and lime leaves. They had spread out and become illegible!

---

[10] A cubit is equivalent to 0.524 m, i.e. $\times 18 = 9.432$ m.

- But, revered Pontiff, haven't our researchers managed to make a smooth paste from the touf[11] that grows in the marshes?

- That's right, Rabou-Nit; it's on these sheets of touf from the river that I'm copying my drawings this time.

- And the formula is good?

- It is; we will be able to reintroduce the writing of the Sacred Texts in due course.

- Perhaps then we can dispense with the need to engrave these writings on the stone of monuments?

- Don't think that, because engraving on lime-coated stone is an absolute necessity. Our Golden Circle must be indestructible and still legible and usable in ten or a hundred millennia! As for the touf, it's subject to the wear and tear of any of the four elements, and it will disappear. But for the time being, it is a gift from Ptah as beneficial as the Great River itself, which allows it to grow. Not only will it be used to write texts, but it is also suitable for nourishment from its roots, and for weaving the fibres of its stem into garments.

- We'll be a great nation again as soon as life returns to normal, O venerated Pontiff. But couldn't you get some help from the architects who are already working on your data?

- Unfortunately, this is impossible! I must remain the sole holder of the formulations and give each of the eight people in charge only the documents relating to their part of the work. Every day, before the sun rises, I'll give them the sheets of paper they need to ensure

---

[11] The touf is obviously papyrus, a plant that grew in the marshes along the banks of the Nile, a miraculous plant that was used for many purposes in the days of the early Egyptians.

the smooth running of the most gigantic project since the Golden Circle was built in our sunken capital.

- How will you resist alone, O Pontiff?

- I'll solve this problem, and each works manager will only know the details relating to the team for which he or she is responsible. As there will be more than three thousand rooms of different sizes and shapes, that will be the real difficulty in coordinating everything without any mistakes! And each of the eight people in charge will have to train his eldest son to carry on with the same task, so on until the Great Work is completed!

- Why not trust one of us too?

- It is not because of a lack of confidence, my friends; it is because it is written that no living being, apart from the Pontiff in office, must know the complete interior of the Golden Circle, for the whole of the double buildings will be equivalent to perfect Knowledge of the Law of the Universe and its unfettered handling. I alone will be the possessor of this Secret during my lifetime, and this construction of Ta-Nout-Ra-Ptah will remain unique in the world because no other mortal will be able to have full access to it, on pain of dying in the corridors from which he will never be able to escape!

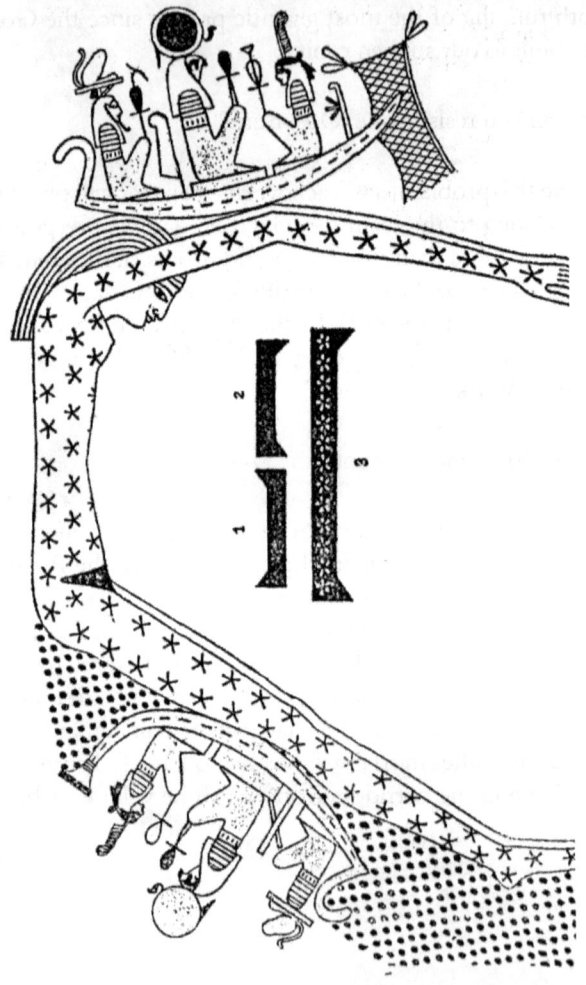

The *message on the previous page, through its symbol, is one of the many fundamental figurations engraved on the walls of the main Egyptian Temples. The importance of this design is extremely simple, because it allows us to reread, without the need for any written text, the entire primordial scene of the* "Great Cataclysm" *that caused Ahâ-Men-Ptah to be swallowed up and Eden to disappear.*

The "Divine Triad" *was at the head of all the Survivors, who under a new retrograde Sun became the* "Survivors of Atlantis", *giving birth through Hor*

(Horus) to a dynasty of Pêr-Ahâ in hieroglyphic, or Pharaohs in Greek, i.e. "Sons of God".

First and foremost is NOUT, the Virgin Queen, mother of Usir (Osiris); having given birth to God's Eldest, she ascended to Heaven where she has protected the multitude of Cadets ever since. Queen NOUT is thus identified with the Milky Way. Here, her body is studded with stars, forming the bridge between East and West, like the "Great Celestial River".

So let's start in the west, where the terrible catastrophe took place. The raging sea has buried all the land on the immense continent, leaving only the "Mandjit" - unsinkable boats designed for survival - on the surface of the water.

In the boat on the left is Ousir, whose head is invisible beneath his bandage, the redness of which symbolises the bull's skin in which he has actually been imprisoned. Symbolically too, the hindquarters of a Lion are placed on the bandages, personifying for all eternity the upheaval that occurred when the Sun passed through the constellation Leo in retrograde position.

Seated next to Usir is Hor, Usir's son, personified by the sparrow hawk, and bearer of the Sun, for on his survival depends the rebirth of the survivors. As he has been seriously wounded and is hanging on by a thread, his life cross, the Antaeus Cross, is bloody, unlike the one held by Iset (Isis), Hor's mother and Usir's wife, which is yellow and the sign of long life.

The three of them form the symbolic "triad", and Iset balances the soul of the survivors on his head, symbolised by a green ostrich feather. (The hieroglyph for the "Divine Parcel for Man" is the drawing of an ostrich feather).

And the Divine Triad is on a "Mandjit" whose oar has even disappeared, and which is floating on the brink of shipwreck, the waters reaching the highest point!

Let's move on to the "Mandjit" on the right, which has made it through the difficult passage, probably with the help of a makeshift sail, fixed archaically! They have reached the Orient bren that the land is called, due to the pivoting of the earth's axis: TA MANA, "The Place of the Sunset". The soul of the world is implanted firmly in the hull, while Ousir has regained his human aspect, but only for a short time, as his red soul sinks into the lion's hindquarters, since the Sun is still in the same constellation. His Antaeus Cross is also red, and Set, his assassin, depicted as a dog, is going to take back what he has already killed.

As for Hor, still wounded, he will land with the new Sun above him and Iset will be in full possession of his means, thanks to his yellow soul and his Cross of the same colour from which a Lotus flower has emerged, a sure sign of the Rebirth of the Elder Hor who will ensure that the Survivors will forever be the race of the Elders, the Sons of God; the Per-Ahâ, or Pharaohs.

CHAPTER II

TA NOUT-RA-PTAH
(THE HEAVENLY PLACE)

> *"Of all the ruins, the most marvellous is Tentyris. It has 180 windows, and every morning the Sun enters through a different window until it reaches the last one, after which it makes the same journey in the opposite direction."*
>
> EL-MAKRISI
> *(Description of Egypt - 1468.)*

> *"The universe is so resplendent with divine poetry only because a divine mathematics, a divine combination of numbers, animates its movements.*
>
> HIS HOLINESS PIUS XI
> *(Last Easter homily).*

As he reached the top of the hill, *Bâ-En-Pou* breathed a sigh of relief. This climb, under *the* sun that was beginning to shine on his tunic, was beyond his years. But what more would he have to endure before being welcomed among the sleeping Blessed of Ahâ-Men-Ptah, who remained forever his first heart, and whom legend was already transforming into everyday language into an abbreviation: Amenta!

The Pontiff did not dwell on this question, for a vast moving panorama stretched out far below his feet. Hundreds of workers had already begun levelling the land marked out in the loop of the river to be used for the construction of the strangest and most gigantic building ever conceived and undertaken by human minds using celestial coordinates. The sight that fascinated and enthralled him was that of an immense beehive buzzing, but in the open air. Thousands of workers were busy below, performing all day long the only gestures they had learnt to take part in this work, without worrying about those of their neighbours.

Soon, thick, taut ropes would precisely delimit the outer perimeter wall around the flattened area. Around the perimeter of this vast esplanade, piles of the most diverse materials were already being piled up, materials that would soon be used to begin the underground foundations.

But first, *Bâ-En-Pou* was to make the actual start of the work official by consecrating the site of Ta Nout-RâPtah, to place it under the triple divine protection to which it was dedicated. In this way, the Golden Circle would proudly bear his name until the end of time. Its triple designation by Ptah, Nut and Ra would ideally make it the Celestial Abode, and astronomically the Double Death, since it would be necessary to separate day from night in order to avoid all possible temptations from any pretender of good intentions.

The Pontiff's greatest task had been to include, in the sequence of the main work, innumerable unforeseen links that would serve as impenetrable locks for anyone attempting to disobey the path planned for the teaching of future initiates. Everything was already compartmentalised and structured on the plans; all that remained was to assemble each of the apparently disordered parts to the next, so that the Golden Circle could be reborn.

The enormous blocks of granite were already being cut, a few days' sail upstream on the river. He would no longer be at the head of the College of High Priests when these masses of stone reached Ta Nout-Râ-Ptah, but the Pontiff knew that from now on the work would follow its course whatever happened. As he closed his eyes, he could already see the sturdy sledges with their large runners, pulled by ever-changing teams, shuttling back and forth between the riverbank and this blessed place, thanks to a smooth road to be built, which would be made slippery with oily river silt spread on the ground, which would stick to the sand as it dried.

Opening his eyes again, the Patriarch returned to the present moment, for the line of priests who had followed him at a respectful distance had passed him by and were descending to prepare for the consecration of 'Ta Nut-Ra-Ptah. Overlooking the shaven heads, he followed in his turn, watched out of the corner of his eye by Tan-Pet, always present to prevent the Master from failing too visibly. But as they descended, An-Nu's tall stature, all girded in white and seemingly solid as a rock, flew over the roughness of the ground! His eyes, half-closed and hidden by thick eyebrows, seemed inexpressive and dispassionate, while an inflexible will carried him irresistibly towards his ultimate goal: to complete the task with which he had been entrusted!

With the new generation advancing by leaps and bounds at the moment, the Future was already taking root in ways that would soon become impossible to define! He absolutely had to complete the religious education of his loved ones before he disappeared! And how could he get them to touch an intangible reality? The Past was irreversible, and the notions of Good and Evil were sometimes so similar that one could easily swarm the other.

After forty centuries of anguish and hardship, the Pontiff knew that the story of Ahâ-Men-Ptah, authentic though it was, was already taking on the trappings of legend and fabrication. After all, isn't lying, in this case, a blessing that preserves the essential Truth?

But *Bâ-En-Pou* once again interrupted his train of thought as he reached the immense esplanade. Silence gradually fell, the workers stopping work to watch the ceremony and listen to the homily of the religious leader!

The Patriarch passed by, impassive, unconcerned about the marks of respect he was the object of, fortifying himself with the unshakeable truth of the dogmas of the Law, which he undertook to make everyone respect, so that the Sons of Light would be reborn before his disappearance.

But it was time to begin. Aided by the Horoscope who had approached him, the Pontiff pulled himself up onto a sandstone boulder, not only to tower over the Priests, but also so that his voice could be heard by the workers scattered across the site. *Bâ-En-Pou* had a quick look satisfied. From this still empty space, the hands of men would bring forth a perfect whole: the *Double House of Life of the "Divine-Mathematical Combinations"*, the Golden Circle, the celestial place: Ta-Nout-Râ-Ptah.

Straightening up proudly, the Pontiff began in a loud voice[12]:

- Let us invoke Ptah, the almighty God of the Beginning, on this particularly important day. Let us also invoke Usir, who has risen to enable us to build this thrice-holy edifice. Let us also invoke Nut, the good Virgin Queen and her daughter Iset, who have been combined under the name of Goddess of Heaven, to keep a special watch over those who will spend their lives studying the meaning of the celestial configurations, the signs of God. Finally, let us invoke Hor, the Elder of the Divine Triad who guided our Ancestors to this earth, so that he may likewise advise the servants of Ptah in their earthly actions on behalf of humans.

Hundreds of chests repeated the invocations in one fervent voice. Slowly, the Pontiff raised his two long arms to Heaven in silent but inspired supplication. The sleeves of his tunic, pulled down to his armpits, revealed the skeletal thinness of this very old servant of the Lord. His voice, however, as it rose again, seemed extra ordinary strong and youthful, every word carried with force to the ears of the most distant worker:

- May the most wise and infinitely good God, who will regulate our new condition as living beings on this blessed earth, deign to

---

[12] The prayer below is taken in its entirety from *The Hymn to the Creator God*, the name given by the Russian Egyptologist W. Golénitscheff to the hieratic papyrus he discovered in Upper Egypt. The beginning of this manuscript indicates that it was *copied* by the scribe of King Thutmose III (of the 18th dynasty) from a very ancient document. It is kept in the Leningrad Museum under the name "Hieratic Papyrus No. 1116".

consider today the work we are undertaking here for His greater Glory and to ensure that His Law is respected.

"For it is He alone who made heaven and earth for our happiness!

"For it is He alone who has pushed back the darkness so that we may become the Sons of Light.

"For it is He alone who made the Breath that animates our Soul.

"Thus the Soul breathed by the Twelve Celestials of the Creator has taken the place of the carnal spirit in a body.

"In this way, Human Life has found its way into our carnal envelopes, along with the Divine Parcel that is the Soul.

"This is why man is a creature of God.

"This is why the Creator also made plants, animals, birds, fish and all things that are in the water, in the air or on the earth, in order to ensure the existence of his Creatures.

"Let no man ever dishonour the model whose image *he* bears, on pain of the worst punishments!

"Let Man eat and drink as other living beings do. But let Man pray and thank God for having made him human. But let man work to be truly human.

"And the Elder, Usir, was the completion of the Creator's Creation.

"And thanks to this, we Cadets will have Peace and Prosperity on Earth, while waiting to be accepted in the Beyond of our earthly life, where we will finally be able to join the Sleeping Blessed, our venerated forebears of the Amenta.

"May the eternal glory of Ptah bathe us all in its Light.

Having completed this traditional part of the sanctification, the Pontiff brought the sleeves of his tunic up to his wrists, before continuing, looking especially at the young classes of future priests:

- Three hundred and sixty generations of Pontiffs, Guardians of the Texts of our Sacred Language, have helped to preserve this Knowledge intact. At every primordial moment of life, without interruption. Over the past five thousand years, they have indicated the favourable designs of the Eternal One, who alone presents the signs to be followed or formally rejected...

The Pontiff let the end of his sentence hang over the heads of the frustrated but attentive listeners. Then he continued in an even louder voice, after beating his chest three times:

- Today, I alone remain the custodian of this extraordinary past of our Elders. I will pass it on, for the sake of the Cadets of the future, to those who will perpetuate our race, in the hope that they will avoid the recurrence of a calamity as appalling as the one that struck our First Heart and wiped it off the face of the Earth once and for all. This is why humanity, which will soon be living under your spiritual tutelage, must imperatively follow the divine commandments according to the precepts that you will teach, and which will be the true reflection of the Law of the Creator. And if, at times, certain Dogmas seem burdensome to teach, never give in to the temptation to ignore them or to modify them according to your own theological conceptions. Each of the Words that make up the Sacred Law comes from God Himself, and each Word of the Word has its strict raison d'être in the place where it is situated!

During the brief silence that allowed him to catch his breath, the Pontiff pointed an index finger over the shorn skulls of the priests in office:

- The intangible and indivisible Law will be bequeathed to your pupils just as you received it, without taking anything away from it, because it will always, everywhere, constitute the indestructible bulwark necessary for the survival of our sons and their great-grandchildren! And so it has been since our origins in Ahâ-Men-Ptah. The horrible experience of those who tried to counterfeit and contravene Divine Law must serve as a lesson to us all! No one should try to make their own law prevail over that of God, because it is impossible for a human being to create what the Creator has placed in the world to ensure your earthly life.

Another short pause allowed the Pontiff to calm his breathing, which had become breathless with sudden oppression. This gave time for the prophetic words of warning to penetrate to the deepest recesses of souls. The old holy man then resumed in a voice that was not cracked, but vibrant:

That is why you will swear, as I did long ago, to obey unconditionally the commandments of Divine Law. That is why you will never forget that your main task as servants of God will be to teach the Cadet people, always and always, the strictest observance of this Faith that our Elders have done everything to pass on to us in its entirety! In simple terms, this is what inspires me at this moment of exceptional gravity: the beginning of the work of the Golden Circle...

The Pontiff made a sweeping gesture with his right hand, sweeping the entire horizon, while everyone unconsciously repeated the two somewhat magical words "Golden Circle". And *Bâ-En-Pou* continued:

- The gigantic school of "Divine-Mathematical Combinations" will emerge thanks to the hard work of all of you. The celestial aspects of this day are the most beneficial, proof that our Elders had absolute mastery in the knowledge of astral combinations. We are entering an era of unprecedented prosperity, which will not be repeated for many years to come. This divine clemency comes to us from the resurrection of Usir, and his accession to the celestial throne at the right hand of Ptah, the place assigned to him in his time under the patronymic of the Celestial Bull. Today, Ra casts his most beneficent rays on our Second Heart, influenced by the one of the Twelve that is in its best position: the Heart of Taurus! This is why, on this thrice-blessed day, right here, our ancient Golden Circle of Ath-Mer l'engloutie will be reborn from its prestigious past, thanks to God and the work of all his creatures. The greatest complex ever created for the understanding of Creation and the mathematical combinations that animate it has already been placed under the protection of Usir, generator of the new multitude, personified in our writings by the Divine Bull. With the Sun now entering the constellation dedicated to it for more than two thousand years as an eternal symbol of gratitude, we will soon be able to rise from our own ashes with the reproduction of all our past, past but very present in our hearts. May Usir, the glorious Son of the Father, intercede with his Creator, who is also ours, so that the Golden Circle, which will not see its inauguration until long after our return to the Beyond of earthly life, resists not only the onslaught of time, but above all that of the carnal envelopes envious and jealous of our civilisation. May the Breath of Ptah and the Twelve protect you all during this life of labour to the greater glory of God! In this way you will attain Eternal Life with the Blessed Sleeping Ones of Ahâ-Men-Ptah. Thus end my words.

This open-air consecration ceremony came to an end. The workers quickly resumed their tasks, returning to a regular, efficient rhythm, making the esplanade once again resemble a vast anthill, with thousands of workers toiling away in a single, perfectly coordinated movement.

The An-Nu, pleased with what he saw, held on tightly to the arm held out to him by the Horoscope to climb down from his sandstone pedestal. Without further ado, the Pontiff beckoned his two companions to follow him:

- There's still time, before the prayer in the sun, check on the state of progress of the celestial vault of the great temple. Let's get going!

For better understanding, we will leave this astronomical visit to the temple of Ta Nout-Râ-Ptah here, to describe in detail this vault, a veritable map of the sky, which has been the subject of so many polemics between the distinguished Members of all the learned institutions throughout the world since 1820, the date on which the sixth copy of this monument was brought back to Paris.[13]

Long before this Era of Taurus began, we have already seen, the idea of reproducing a terrible event that had taken place in the distant past, but was to remain eternally in the memory of mankind, was the subject of deep reflection and meditation on how to represent it in such a way that it would remain eternally engraved in people's minds. Among the descendants of an Elder people who rightly ascribed to themselves such a degree of Wisdom and Knowledge, the very conception of such a monument had to be equal to their Knowledge.

So, to make it easy to understand, the very basis of the figurative interpretation system was the Lion. This boundary would appear to be impassable for those whom God's wrath might eventually wipe off the face of the Earth a second time. This perpetual fear of a cataclysmic restart that could this time irreparably destroy Ath-KâPtah, the second Mother Country, was the fundamental idea behind what arbitrarily became the Zodiac in the 19th century.

So this planisphere, or more precisely a map of the sky for a specific day, 27 July 9792 BC, is the exact projection of a section of the celestial sphere. From this point of view alone, the few defects that appear on the sixth copy in our possession are minor. Let's not forget that there were more than four thousand years between the construction of the first building and the one that still exists today, dating back to the Ptolemies of the pre-Christian centuries.

To represent this extraordinary and exceptional event, the circle features three main series of figurations, the most important of which is obviously that of the twelve zodiacal constellations. They are remarkably arranged in a spiral. This is a double indication. The first is that the hieroglyphic sign of Creation is a spiral. The second, which follows on from this, is that Creation is an eternal restart, but

---

[13] In a historical work on this subject, *Le Zodiaque de Dendérah*, the author recounts all the ups and downs of this monument, to be published by Ed. Omnia Veritas.

not in a closed circle. Creation evolves in a space-time that is perpetually renewed after a semblance of an end.

The first engraving is of a Lion on a Mandjit (the saving boat), the twelfth being Cancer, located slightly above the Lion's head. And their relative positions in relation to the sky are perfectly assigned, since Cancer is to the south and Leo's head to the north.

It is therefore Leo, with the Sun rising in the east rather than the west, that opens the march of the procession of the Twelve. Placed, as it is, under Cancer, it reopens an advance in time, but backwards in space after the station effected by this solstice improvised by God. There is no doubt that this representation of the constellation Cancer indicates the retrograde advance of the Sun.

In its primary figurative symbolism, the renewal of the sun from the other hemisphere and its reversed declination perfectly illustrate the catastrophic event that has occurred. What's more, the celestial navigation completed northwards by the star of the day is reinforced by the drawing of Cancer following that of the Twins Usir and Set (later to become Gemini) in the form of a Crab moving backwards.

The first figure is therefore the Lion, standing firmly on a Mandjit symbolised by the serpent of the ancient impious multitude, and carrying on its curved tail, clinging to its hair, the image of a small woman representing the Cadets born of the survivors of the cataclysm. This is, of course, Iset, mother of Horus, the Eldest son of all the future survivors of the Second Heart. Next comes Nut, the Virgin Queen who gave birth to Usir and thus justified her enthronement under the patronymic of the constellation Virgo. She holds an ear of wheat in her hands, symbolising the divine seed she carries within her, which is already following her like a shadow, in human form with the head of a bull. The crescent of the setting sun, that of the Sleeping Blessed, is on his head, and he is holding in his left hand the jackal-faced staff, symbolising Set the assassin, ultimately subservient to his Elder.

The third drawing represents the Scales of Divine Justice. It alone can weigh the actions of each person in all fairness. It was thanks to the scales that for more than two millennia after this first engraving, there was virtually no war, with every conflict being settled during the month dedicated to the scales, before a stone dedicated to this purpose and bearing a golden balance around which sat twenty-two judges.

Scorpio, which follows it in the sequence of the twelve, owes its name to the last Nar-Mer king, who unified the two fratricidal clans. Its time is one of the shortest in the Great Year, so there's not much more to say about this constellation. The same cannot be said for the next constellation.

Sagittarius, a monster half animal, half man, ready to shoot an arrow from his bow, symbolises for all eternity the divine warning against the actions of the sun worshippers, the descendants of Set the assassin, without any faith, and their disobedience to the Law of the Almighty Lord of Eternity.

Capricorn follows him, lying down but about to stand up again, as can be seen from the carriage of his head and the tension in one of the supporting legs. On his back is Horus, shown with his hawk-like head, presenting the staff he is holding as a victor, the insignia of his victory over his uncle Set.

The man walking behind is holding a vase in each of his two hands, with the water flowing out in a sawtooth pattern. This is the water-verse, or the constellation Aquarius. The Masters of Measure and Number symbolise this presentation with the image of the Creator opening the floodgates of heaven either to drown his Creation under a second cataclysm, or to flood away the sins of the world to bring about a golden age accessible to all survivors.

Which will it be? The descendants of Usir or those of Set? The two perfectly identical fish on the planisphere, linked together by a cord but separated from each other by a hieroglyphic ideogram representing three broken lines, in other words the emblem of the flood, give an important revelation: that it will be those who finally respect the Knowledge of the Law who will have their lives saved, whether they are descendants of Usir or simply survivors of Set.

Aries, which is precisely the sign of the Sun-worshipping usurpers, the symbol of the abhorred Amun whose capital Thebes was for nearly two millennia, is shown looking backwards, lying in the opposite direction to his historical march, that is to say looking towards the East and not towards Ahâ-Men-Ptah and the Elders, and the two figures immediately below his body will not be able to help him overcome the countless remaining difficulties.

The Bull, caracoling in his wake, clearly turns his head towards the East, thus presenting the concavity of his horns towards the setting sun where the Elders of Ahâ-Men-Ptah rest. This celestial bull is most animated, seeming to dart northwards and out of the spiral circle of the Twelve as if it were part of all the living worlds and beyond.

For Gemini, the Masters in charge of symbolism have presented a picture of four figures, the two main ones holding hands and being Ousir and his wife Iset. The twins, on the other hand, are relegated to the bottom of the engraving of Aries, as explained on the previous page. This substitution must be seen as an unshakeable desire to recall the shame of the fratricides that lasted for nearly five millennia before reaching the land of the second homeland.

Finally, Cancer appears just above Leo, as mentioned at the beginning. It should also be noted that the first representation of this constellation was a scarab, which later became a crab. It was not until the Greco-Roman era that it took the name Cancer.

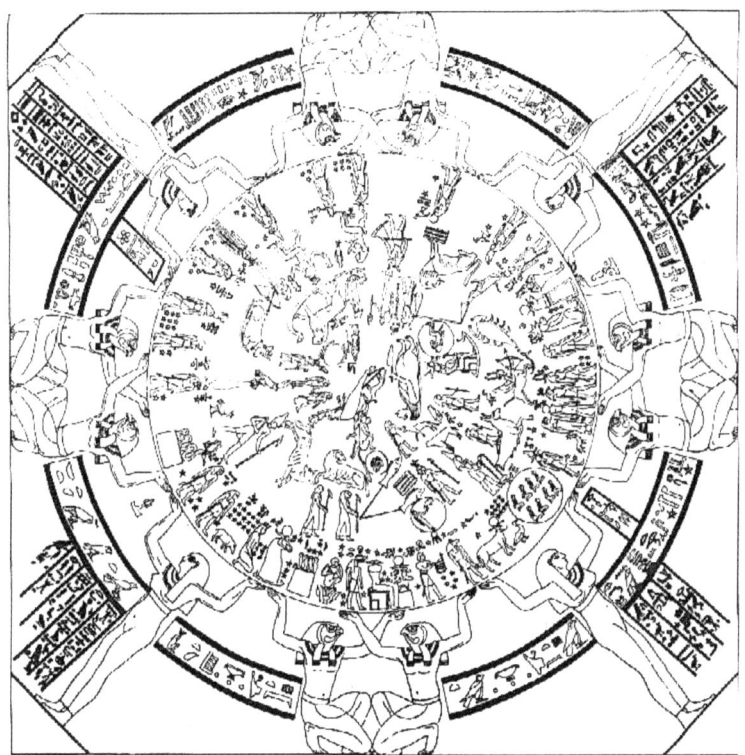

Here is the Denderah planisphere as it was brought back to France to France by M. Lelorrain in 1822.

The space inscribed by the Twelve contains a large number of figures. The most important is the central figure, a very large animal that is part crocodile, part hippopotamus, an animal that Egyptologists have described as "typhonian" because it symbolises the most peaceful but also the most dangerous of the gods: God himself. Ptah the One. He is depicted holding a large cutlass, the same one used by Set, but this is merely a vengeful representation of the engravers, who are human par excellence! For in his beneficent harmony, Ptah had in mind only total earthly equilibrium for his creatures. And that's what the central figure is all about.

Two other circular series of hieroglyphic figures complete the description of the Twelve to give it a precise date, with Sep'ti our Sirius, the equivalent of Orion, in the Big Dipper, and their respective positions calculated with the help of one of the thirty-six decans broken down at the bottom of the third series.

The large outer circle is supported by four groups of men with hawks' heads, symbolising the descendants of the four sons of Horus. Isis stands in the middle of each gap between the groups, supporting the medallion. The explanation in the Sacred Language can be read along her legs in several vertical lines. It is interesting to note that, to avoid having to carry a lot of extra weight when transporting the medallion to France, Mr Lelorrain simply cut out the planisphere, leaving the giant figure of Nut in place, giving the astronomical direction of the monument with her outstretched hands. Mr Lelorrain also sawed through the zigzags in the drawing below, which, as he explained on his return to Paris, were of no importance! Now, if we know that one 'zigzagged' or broken line hieroglyphically signifies a movement of water, that three indicate a flood like that of the Nile, and that five announce a deluge of water, it is clear that eight or nine of these 'zigzagged' lines describe a great catastrophe involving water: the Great Cataclysm that buried the Elder Heart, Ahâ-Men-Ptah, as described in the Denderah sky chart.

Let's return now to the historical period that preceded the arrival of the first Elder officially described in the "modern" Annals: Mena, or Menes in Greek phonetics. It can be described romantically as the Renaissance.

CHAPTER III

THE RENAISSANCE

> *"The labyrinth is made up of twelve courtyards surrounded by walls. Their flats are double; there are fifteen hundred underground and fifteen hundred above. I have visited the rooms above and I speak of them as a witness, with certainty."*
> HERODOTUS
> *(History of Egypt).*

> *"I will mention an underground passage discovered by chance in the southern part of the temple at Denderah. Its entrance was well hidden by a movable stone decorating the room. It gave access to a series of corridors and chambers where initiation tests were to be performed.*
> VISCOUNT EMMANUEL DE ROUGE
> *(Report to the Minister of Public Education) May 1864.*

The centuries passed without a single second's delay at their own pace, and the last year of Sep'Ti[14], without its public countdown, would soon come to an end. Regular Time would then resume its course within the Second Heart, for human hearts.

The Pontiff Méri-Hotep[15] shook his head to put on a brave face, more moved than he would have liked. He was no longer strong enough to cope with all the preparatory work in the field. But what

---

[14] Sep'ti is the star Sirius, which became Sothis in Greek. The Sothian year, or "Year of God", lasts 1461 solar years. More than three hundred years have passed since Bâ-En-Pou, and the calendar will be re-established on the first day of year 1, i.e. 4,244 BC, as we shall see later, by the son of Menes.

[15] Literally: "the Aimé-Pacifique".

was the point of rebelling against the simple banality of life on earth? He had to concentrate his last reserves of energy on translating certain more delicate celestial configurations into the concrete aspects of daily life, so that they would occupy the central part of the "Golden Circle", the part that precisely delimits the Sages from the initiates, and which could hold the key to understanding, giving access to the vital centre of Knowledge.

For several months now, the Pontiff had been assisted in his various tasks by Nou-Kaï and Hady-Pet, two first-class priests, probably the most erudite of all those of their generation. Having no sons of his own, which was his perpetual sadness, it would certainly be one of these two that the College of High Priests would appoint to succeed him before long.

The private prayer room had just emptied and he beckoned the two clerics to wait for him. They nodded in unison, smiling modestly as they had no intention of slipping away in the absence of the An-Nu.

They in turn left the Holy Place, following the Pontiff. The sun was shining brightly and serenely on the horizon, as usual. The religious building had not yet been completed, as the other more pressing works were taking up all the workers' time. Here, the scaffolding remained unoccupied, and the engravings and paintings on the ceilings had barely begun. This was not the case outside, where the surrounding wall surrounding the immense esplanade was full of activity! On three superimposed levels, clinging tightly to hundreds of ropes, sanders, engravers and, just below them, stonemasons were busily engaged in their precise tasks.

The three priests always admired it after the monks' morning mass. And every day, the Pontiff would stop in front of one of the four monumental doors to see if there were any writing errors in the hieroglyphic texts, but he hadn't found any yet!

Then they stopped with one accord as they crossed the threshold of this door to judge all the work they had before them.

The west-east axis of the sacred horizon, the one that linked the Past of the West to the Eternity of the East, stretching its forty-eight thousand cubits[16] of Divine Way amidst the superstructures that were already taking shape, giving a foretaste of what the giant complex of the "Golden Circle" would be, This House of the Universe, still very heterogeneous in terms of the surprising diversity of the hundreds of low walls that appeared here and there, of varying heights, appearing to have been erected at random, but whose every mathematical and geometric detail had been carefully studied, as the three priests could attest!

The lower half of this structure would take shape and form before being completed and covered with the ceiling slab, which would form the floor of the upper half. The chambers of the "Nocturnal Mathematical Combinations" would disappear into the night, supervised by the Moon. Each of the astral aspects would occupy a different room under the floor, linked to the next by a corridor that would change and move with the hours and days. Numerous underground passages, already covered with black granite blocks, were traps and traps for those who didn't observe the strict mathematical laws!

The Pontiff smiled at this thought, for what was being said on the subject would certainly prevent any "onlookers" from getting too close! His gaze shifted to the perimeter formed by the Sacred Lake. It formed the perspective that closed off the western horizon and was even more important than the complex being built, forming an immense basin, the lower level of which had been reached. The final foundations were being laid where the two square-based foundations of the "Loved Ones-who-descend-the-

---

[16] The Egyptian cubit, of which several standard measurements have been found intact, is very precisely calculated at 0.524 m. For the west-east axis of the Divine Way, this is $48,000 \times 0.524 = 8.384$ km. It should be noted that around sixty kilometres from the Dendera site is the triumphal way of Aries-Amon, the solar god, which links Karnak to Luxor, and which measures exactly twice as long!

Light[17] " would be built. Here too, myriads of workers, like conscientious ants, were busy with the sole aim of carrying out the tasks for which they had been trained. This inland sea would complete the true panorama of this holy place, giving it back an ancient aspect of previous civilisation. It would make it possible to harness the waters of the great river and irrigate the land in times of drought.

But the brief moment of ecstasy and relaxation ended with the arrival of the architects in charge of the work, who approached the trio of priests with slow steps, as if measuring their efforts to prove that they were also specialists in Numbers. The arms of most of the eight men were loaded with scrolls and flat sheets of papyrus, newly treated to be completely smooth. The scripture recreated according to Tradition, but in an even more imaginative form, surrounded the drawn lines of the plans with incalculable series of numbers and letters! It would be possible to officially reintroduce the current use of hieroglyphics at the appointed time, after a deliberate oversight since the sinking of AhâMen-Ptah.

As they did every morning, the eight architects came to their orders, no longer bothered by the lack of foresight in scheduling the work. They had accepted this way of doing things, just as their fathers and grandfathers had done before them! It was all the easier for them, in spite of their heavy responsibilities, because there were no delays, no clashes, in the pursuit and sequencing of each day's work! The heads of the works awaited the Pontiff's orders, attentive to any changes that might be decided at the last minute: but they never came! Everything was meticulously prepared!

The gleaming robes of these men, very visible under their fine tunics of unbleached linen, flashed red under the rays of the sun, showing everyone the red colour inherent in the high office they held in the professions of mathematics or astronomy. They themselves were followed by a swarm of scribes, reed quills stuck

---

[17] This is the hieroglyphic name. Pyramid is a word that is all the more abstract for the fact that it means nothing in either Greek or Hebrew!

in their hair and on the calames they carried on one shoulder, while their other arm collapsed under the weight of voluminous masses of papyrus.

When they came within a few steps of the Pontiff, they bowed respectfully in perfect harmony, before the Priest, head of all the works, spoke:

- Greetings to you, O venerated Pontiff; may the peace of Ptah remain eternally upon your august person. Conti nue de veiller sur ta santé et de surveiller avec autant de succès la poursuite des travaux du Grand Ouvrage! For we need your wise counsel for many years to come... Are you satisfied, O MeriHotep?

- My satisfaction could only be human, PenAfet, and this work is intended to serve God's Creation! But it seems to me that the Eternal One would have every reason to be satisfied with the eagerness of his creatures to serve him so promptly and so faithfully! He sees everything from above, and he knows that the goodwill of each worker is essential to the success of the work.

- Thank you, O venerable Pontiff, for these kind words. We are indeed nearing completion of the first part of the future Living House of the Golden Circle. We are finishing the work underground.

- It's a very good thing indeed, but it seems to me that the hardest part will still be dealing with the buildings above...

- This is not so certain, because the work will be less exhausting. Engraving the texts of the celestial configurations will just be a matter of getting used to it. However, it's true that there will be more work: couldn't you get other workers, even untrained ones, to help out wherever extra hands are needed? That way I could free up some of them to learn engraving or drawing...

- The builders of the temples in the north, who returned to their distant provinces after the last celebrations commemorating our unification, are due to send us several hundred of their workers before the waters of the Great River rise again. They will arrive in the large flat boats they are lending us.

- Why such kindness from them ?!

- This is one of those official exchanges of courtesies agreed at the last Joint Council held over the festive period. You are no doubt aware of the tenacious will of our Pêr-Ahâ: the Divine Nar-Mer, whose strict authority has never wavered.

The Chief Architect couldn't help but laugh outright:

- Who doesn't know all the acts of bravery and feats of arms against those in the North who already wanted to break up the union! But I hadn't heard anything about this exchange decision.

- There were so many takings during these five days of celebrations! Our Scorpion-King, as he has decided to call himself with his emblem featuring this animal, likes to get things done quickly, not to be annoyed and above all to pique the interest of these ex-rebels who are so far removed from his authority! To bring these distant brothers closer to us, he has carried out a number of prestigious operations, including getting us to lend several of their heavy boats to transport our largest blocks of stone from upriver to here. In exchange, we agreed to train some of their good workers as engravers who had acquired the technique of working on very hard stone.

- When will they arrive, O venerated Pontiff?

- They shouldn't be long now, as the star of Isis[18], blessed be she, which has been appearing for the last four days, heralds the start of the flood.

- Will they be staying long for this apprenticeship?

- We'll have it for at least five full moons. As long as the river remains high, the men will stay with us. And their boats will bear the weight of our biggest blocks, those destined to pave the first level of the Golden Circle.

The Chief Architect bowed his head in approval and respect before this admirable old man, who was doing everything according to a meticulously preconceived plan to ensure that the work would continue without a hitch. He frankly expressed his satisfaction, almost forgetting his quality:

- This is perfect, O Pontiff! I couldn't have drawn up a better work plan! We're going to use these northerners to the best of our urgent needs, while teaching them our method of engraving.

- Your teams will grow in value Pen-Afet! For today, are they ready to descend? Do you have extra supplies for them?

- Here too, you have prepared everything meticulously, as usual, O Meri-Hotep. The keepers of your silos have already carried out your orders to send us the extra onions and garlic we requested. This supply is more than enough to keep our meals invigorated until the task is completed. The first day of meticulous work begins tomorrow in the seventy-two main rooms below. With the extra spices delivered, it's shaping up to be a good start!

---

[18] It is, of course, the star Sirius, which was given the name Isis and became the "Lady of Heaven". In this way, she gives rhythm to the march of time. Hieroglyphics would later use her face as an asterism in astronomy to indicate Sirius.

- How many specialists will you have?

- Each of the eight teams will be made up of six hundred engravers.

- Is this enough?

- We will maintain the planned pace, especially if other men from the north come to help us. The workers will not overlap, as they will be distributed between all the parts that will concern the "Fixes" of the night suit rooms. As a certain amount of time is needed to adapt to the special conditions of working underground, this number will be just about sufficient, even with the new arrivals.

- Didn't you try to improve the power of sunlight entering the basement?

- The number of bronze mirrors treated to reflect the sun's rays cannot be increased, O Pontiff. Wherever possible, reflectors have been placed, judiciously distributed so that the light does not blind the workers.

- Everything's just fine! Once again, there's no need to change anything in our work plan. The forecast plans and calculations are still valid. We will remain on this basis for another ten days. The time needed for our Horoscopes to complete their first observations of the engravings that will appear on the lower walls of the Golden Circle.

- In that case, O venerable Pontiff, please allow us to leave you and go about our business. We need to keep a watchful eye on you at all times!

- Well done; go about your particular work, men of great worth. May Ptah protect you and illuminate the path that your Wisdom will follow. May your spirits be imbued with the additional strength that your arms may lack. Go forth!

A new greeting, this time a general one, bowed the torsos of the red-robed wearers as the scribes prostrated themselves to the ground. After this, everyone dispersed in small groups to their various headquarters, from where they would ensure that the works being erected continued to run smoothly and that the engraving began in the rooms on the lower level.

Satisfied with this morning's inspection, which promised action and beneficial technical prowess, the Pontiff beckoned his two collaborators to come closer:

- Without further ado, let's get back to the site dedicated to the "Good Lady"[19]. I can't wait to see if the plaster covering the ceiling tiles is finished. The celestial paintings could be sketched out.

- You must also take all steps today to ensure that the ornaments of the Holy of Holies are rigorously executed, O venerated Pontiff.

- So many orders to carry out! Will I still have enough of the vital force that sustains me?

- Surely, O Meri-Hotep: for many years to come! But don't you want a litter to carry you to the temple? It's a long way back and it's hot!

- But it's going downhill, Hapy-Pet! I'm not completely senile yet, despite my advanced age, for not understanding your eagerness! My legs are still quite capable of carrying me for a few extra efforts. Walking never frightened them!

As soon as Nou-Kaï heard An-Nu's first sharp words about his friend and colleague, he went off to find a large branch to support the old man. He returned quickly, carrying an improvised cane. As

---

[19] It is one of the thousand usual names for Isis and Nut, who are combined in the same Grace. This has been the case throughout the ages of adoration. This was also the case with the Virgin Mary, whose ten thousand names are reminiscent of a polytheistic faith (Our Lady of the Storms, of the Snows, of the Spring, etc.).

he held it out to the Patriarch without a word, he heard the latter say in an exasperated tone, but probably against himself:

- As I have several explanations to give you both, I'll forget the length of them as I talk to you. Thank you for your attention Nou-Kaï. We'd better hurry if we want to get to the temple before Ra's hot rays have reduced us to the state of grilled meat!

The three monks set off at once, descending cending along the same route, albeit a more crowded one. At this late hour of the morning, it was being travelled by incessant convoys of sledges heavily laden with granite blocks.

Taking what he hoped was an alert step forward, the An Nu felt that the time for self-pity had passed. He no longer wanted to think about the vital forces that were escaping from every pore of his skin, too quickly for his liking to allow him to reach the end of his heavy responsibility. Would he be able to decide for himself which of his two companions he would present to the College of High Priests as his successor? When the Pontiff, who had preceded him to the supreme post, had appointed him, he had felt swollen with pride. But over the years, his shoulders had stooped. At the moment, he felt smaller than any of the billions of grains of sand he was treading on. Sixty-eight times since his consecration, the sun had begun its journey again, which showed just how old he was! Who would replace it?

With a resigned sigh, he left this agonising question hanging in the air, hoping that Ptah, in his benevolence, would provide the answer. Méri-Hotep preferred to soliloquise mid-voice, so as to be heard by his two travelling companions, as if they had been following his train of thought all along:

- The years are bending my body towards its final resting place. But I will manage to keep it until the end of my task. When I recall the hours of my true youth, my only moments of childish joy, I realise how rare they were! Very early on, like all my friends, I had to learn part of the Holy Texts, repeating them over and over again, so as not to forget them or change anything. This made me serious before my time. I even aged faster than others, and perhaps that's why I became a Pontiff quite young!

The Patriarch nodded, moved by these distant memories that were flooding back into his mind. He made a great effort not to give in to his emotion and to keep his voice cold and firm. He raised his coarse cane, in turn towards one or other of his companions, before repeating:

- You're lucky, since you're from a generation after mine! Our Second Heart will soon be reborn, with Scripture, the Law, our advanced techniques and our Knowledge of God's decrees. You will no longer suffer the crushing slavery that has been my daily lot. The rebirth of our Motherland on this second earth will sweep away all our past fears! However, I do remember some less unpleasant moments, such as when my mother used to come and kiss me goodnight and give me a handful of fresh dates, as succulent as they were. Instead of closing my eyes, I used to sit down under a big leafy tree to savour them. I took the opportunity to watch the sun 'slip' behind the distant horizon and the moon 'rise' on the other side. I learnt so much by observing nature! At the time, I had no idea that I would become the Pontiff, head of the religious order of Ptah, whom the people venerate almost as much as Nar-Mer, their Pêr-Ahâ. It seems so long ago now, and yet so vivid in my memory! One of you will soon replace me, and your task will be much easier than mine has been. The rebirth of a country as well as its people is an event most blessed by God. The Renaissance of the Second Heart will last forever...

Méri-Hotep stopped talking once more to avoid sinking into melancholy. He lost himself in new thoughts about this long-awaited Renaissance, so ardently sought and prepared for by his predecessors and himself. He was indifferent to the expressions of respect he received as he walked along. Did these good people of hard-working labourers even realise that Ahâ-Men-Ptah, the land of the Ancestors, their "Heart", was about to rise from its ashes? And the Pontiff resumed thinking about this "Elder Heart", enigmatic and engulfed, which was being reborn to throb everywhere around it and in all things, thus manifesting the indestructible and eternal order of the Creator. He continued:

- Our ancestors were all wiped out, swept beneath surface of the waters, by this almighty God who was moved by a righteous and fierce anger against the hearts of his earthly creatures, which now beat only to do evil! Ptah attacked the carnal envelopes, but not the Divine Parcels. The Souls went to the Kingdom of the Blessed, for they had not been conceived for such misfortune. But hearts are only organs of flesh, like the ears, eyes, or feet that carry us. They should be made to beat in unison with each other, not to tear each other apart! For a man's heart is like that of a ram, a gazelle or a bull. They all have a single identical function, and in the same irreversible sense: to give rhythm to the march of Creation, following the flow of time throughout life on Earth. If they beat faster one day or another, it's under the effect of sudden joy, or under the impulse of terror. So how do humans differ from animals? In the vitalisation of hearts by spirits. And here too, there will have to be a rebirth of Souls, to remind them of their duties!

The Pontiff took a few steps silently, looking at their size as if to gauge their significance. This was very difficult to teach, and he had given it up some time ago in the face of the sneers of several Masters of Measurement and Number! I wish he had persevered in this path, because the intuition he would have liked to develop in certain gifted students remained imperceptible in his two companions.

Faced with their silence, he continued:

- Human beings possess thought, and therefore a soul, which alone is capable of celestial survival. This is the only difference, albeit an enormous one, between us bipedal humans and our four-legged brothers. When a carnal envelope comes to an end and the heart stops beating the rhythm of life, only the one that possesses a Divine Parcel, a Soul, can allow it to make its way towards the Kingdom of the Redeemed, and even then, according to very precise rites and the most rigorous conditions of passage! By living according to the commandments of the Law of the Creator, you can unquestionably cross the frontier of the Beyond without damage to your earthly life. It's not for nothing that the Elders bequeathed us Knowledge! And through this immeasurable Knowledge, we are linked with their Souls. There is a real, tangible link that has been created across the two lands: the Englished and this one, which will soon be Ath-Kâ-Ptah: I Second-Heart! That's why I know we must follow the teachings of our Fathers and their ancestors, the Elders, for the wise Words they have passed on to us are the fruits of the most beautiful experience lived before this appalling catastrophe, by the Divine Parcels themselves! This is why we must apply all the precepts of our teaching with the utmost rigour, changing absolutely nothing.

Interrupting his harangue to catch his breath, the Pontiff and his companions stopped at the edge of the construction site of the small temple preceding that of the "Lady of Heaven" and dedicated to Horus, the Elder of Osiris and Isis. The three clerics moved aside to make way for two large sledges with runners, firmly tied together and supporting an enormous block of black granite almost eight metres wide and four metres high. This imposing mass commanded respect for the work it had required. It was this block that, engraved, would represent the splendid graphics of Horus the Pure, personifying him in the guise of a hawk. It was not only a vigilant bird par excellence, but also a fierce protector of its nest!

Five groups of sixteen men toiled on ropes as big as their hands, slung over their shoulders[20]. A foreman was chanting the cadence, modulating two notes as he banged on a hollow wooden sounding board. Two other men ran ahead of the extraordinary convoy to pour out their jugs full of water. These were constantly renewed by other carriers of this precious liquid, making the shuttle to the river.

---

[20] These ropes, several of which have been found, are actually larger than the wrist. They are made of tightly woven papyrus fibres. They have been dated to over 7,000 years ago by the Institute of Egypt in Cairo, and confirmed by the Chicago Institute to within 240 years, i.e. 4,760 BC.

This practice had the dual advantage of ensuring better grip with the ground under the skids therefore easier gliding, while preventing the skids from producing sparks by causing them to burn due to the weight of several hundred tonnes of cargo!

At this magnificent sight, the Pontiff could not hide his satisfaction. The meagre effort and coordinated joint action were so well orchestrated to avoid the slightest difficulty and superfluous fatigue that all the rope-pullers nodded respectfully and smiled at him. No one complained, all too happy to be working for the greater glory of God and the eternal salvation of their souls.

Shortly after resuming their walk, the three priests passed through the monumental gateway leading to the forecourt of the Temple of the Lady of Heaven. The area that would become the esplanade was cluttered with materials of all kinds. But they could already make out the monument that would soon become the finest religious building in the Second Heart.

Queen Nut could already take satisfaction in contemplating the reflections of her face at the top of the sixteen colonnades at the entrance to the temple. The smiling, peaceful face could only bring the fullness and serenity of inner peace to anyone who gazed upon it before praying. And the reverence in which she continued to be held could be seen in the perfection of the smallest details of the little folds at the corners of her mouth, clearly visible in the stonecutters' engravings.[21]

Meri-Hotep understood that no one would ever again question the supremacy of the Divine Nut. In their mad attempts to dominate the Earth by using the vault of heaven, humans would break down body and soul under Nut's sway! It will be she who

---

[21] The first temple at Denderah (Ta NOUT-Râ-Ptah) was dedicated to Queen Nut. Its figuration was then attributed to her daughter!set (Isis), to whom was superimposed her hieroglyphic name HATHOR, or "Heart of Horus", i.e.: mother of Horus, hence: ISIS. Here again, Egyptologists have turned her into several goddesses to justify a non-existent polytheism!

supervises the teaching. And in all the halls, while she will bring her protection by extending her arms over students and novices, her feet, which will touch the ground, will drive the impious into deep oblivion. The Pontiff saw all the stages of Knowledge in a strikingly short space of time, with all the effective means of protection! Nut had inspired him, and he now knew what to say to the priest in red, head of the celestial works in this temple.

The last Queen of Amenta thus gave her tacit consent to the safeguarding of the entire heritage of the Elder Usir, her son. The mysteries of Heaven had been revealed to her so that they could be passed on in their entirety to the Cadets of the Second Heart. This was the Renaissance, and it would happen.

Giving a sharp blow with the stick he had kept, the Patriarch signalled that it was time to set off and continue their inspection of the port before going to rest.

He took the opportunity to repeat in a low voice the theme that was so close to his heart:

- I'll be leaving satisfied with the work I've accomplished, and whoever succeeds me will simply have to follow the path that has been laid out for me. This thrice-sanctified place will become the magnet for all future populations in search of Knowledge. Even those who only get a snippet, true or false, will consider themselves satisfied and return to sow the seed in their distant lands! But if this brings confusion to their unhealthy minds, let it never happen in this Second Heart, for Knowledge is one and all at once. The Golden Circle will be an eternal safeguard. With all its dependencies and warnings, such as the one on the sky chart of the dreadful day of the Great Cataclysm, this consecrated site will justify the first Words of the Ritual of the Beyond of Life, which will soon also appear in writing:

When all the Words of God concerning the annihilation of Ahâ-Men-Ptah have been fulfilled, rebuild the Golden Circle in the designated place in the Promised Land, so that the Law may shine eternally for new generations.

After a short silence and a sigh, Méri-Hotep continued:

- But by way of conclusion, I just wonder whether we won't sooner or later return to another reproduction of a similar catastrophe, because the soul is so made that it forgets its worst misfortunes only to remember them on the day they reappear! And then it's too late to change anything in the general movement of the celestial Universe of God, the Creator!

Chapter IV

THE GOLDEN CIRCLE

"Herodotus, in Book 2, described 12 halls and 3,300 chambers, half underground and half above ground. And if it is a forgivable blunder for ancient authors, such as Pliny and Mela, who never set foot in Egypt, what are we to think of Herodotus and Strabo, who assumed that there were 4 labyrinths, only one of which was in this Kingdom? Here, the largest is independent of the other two. And if it is natural to oppose the authority of one historian to the torrent of others, my reasoning is without reply, for I myself have seen the three labyrinths, of which I visited the largest: that was on 20 July".

FATHER CL. SICARD s.j.
*(Unpublished manuscript
on the History of Egypt). - 1718.*

"This monument was well worth arousing the curiosity of our modern travellers. Two great scholars have tried to find its location. They are d'Anville and Gibert. They took advantage of the precious map that we owe to Father Claude Sicard. I have also benefited from their writings; perhaps other researchers will benefit from my research."

CITIZEN DAVID LE ROY
*(Memorandum read at the Institut on 28
Floréal of the year V.)*

"Forty-two solar revolutions ago, I assumed the weighty responsibility of Supreme Servant of God. When the venerated Pontiff Meri-Hotep was called back to the Blessed Ones who were waiting to welcome him with all the ceremony due to the holy man he was, I already knew that the Golden Circle would be completed under my priesthood. Since yesterday, all the structural work has been completed. There will be no more boulders to transport, no more sand to remove from the depths, no more calculations to make regarding the location of the various movable walls. The whole mechanism is in place!

As the An-Nu *Meri-nut* paused, a murmur went round the priests assembled in the great assembly hall of the temple of Hor, the beloved son of Usir. This religious edifice, smaller than the one dedicated to the "Lady of Heaven", was completely finished and, thanks to its annexes, served as a "House of Life" for all the teachings.

For the most part, these pupils were still in the prime of life, since they only wore the third-class robes of the College, and their instruction in the Sacred Language, Hieroglyphics, had been more advanced, focusing especially for them on anaglyphs and double-possibility ideograms, since they were charged with serving Ptah in an entirely different way from preaching in a holy building. These thirty religious were destined to direct the engravings of the Divine Mathematical Combinations on the walls of the twelve main lower corridors. This very special work had required a long apprenticeship, the end of which they were only now seeing.

The Pontiff was very pleased with the progress of the work, as well as with the skill of the workers. The priests in charge of the work in the Golden Circle were increasingly aware of the heavy responsibility that fell to them. Each in his own sphere, they took their task very much to heart.

The grandeur of this room inspired salutary reflection, and the High Priest, as he gazed at this assembly of shaven heads, saw every detail of the engravings on the pillars and walls, reminding everyone of the Holy Scriptures and the history of the Elders, their ancestors, creatures of God.

A single door made of thick sycamore wood closed off this room, making it completely soundproof. It was framed by a rectangular lintel on which were engraved the three primordial scenes of the rebirth of the survivors of the "First Heart of God", with the Mandjit, the sacred boats, in the foreground. The Divine

Triad was thus honoured for all the self-sacrifice it had shown in enabling the rebirth of the multitude.

Letting out a sigh, Méri-Nout furtively wondered whether everything that was being done to allow another generation of wrongdoers to take over would be understood. How many times would simple reality be distorted to suit selfish and venal interests! But it was time to end this homily so that everyone could get on with their work, so that the spark of truth would remain. With a deep breath, the An-Nu continued:

- May Ptah, the most wise God, who imposes a precise function on us and our work on this earth, now receive our fervent and unanimous prayer. May he help us on this memorable day to move on to the final phase of the work on this gigantic astronomical complex, the Golden Circle. May he give me the strength to steer this enterprise to its conclusion and to complete the formulations of all the Divine Mathematical Combinations so that the Law of the Universe in perpetual motion is engraved in its smallest details in order to re-establish Harmony between Heaven and Earth for Eternity.

"Already, the Golden Circle surrounds the bodies of the buildings, like the Celestial Belt which concentrates the influences of the Twelve in its thousands of astral combinations. Soon, our Golden Belt will draw into its bosom, through its mineral influence, the most beneficial rays into its receptacles. Everything is ready to complete this sacred work on schedule, with the inscriptions that will form the ultimate teaching of Knowledge, the only guarantor of Peace. Peace will remain illusory until our two brother peoples decide to become one: God's chosen people!

"Only a Covenant with the Eternal, sealed by our unification, will ensure a universally good and peaceful life. For the happiness and perfection of the creatures we are here on earth are necessary for the Creator to ensure, at the end of the carnal envelope in its place on earth, the passage of its divine particle beyond the invisible but real frontier, towards the Kingdom of the Blessed Redeemed of the Amenta. Never forget that the Man of millions of future generations will continue to doubt his own origin, if we do not already take all the indispensable precautions to keep him firmly within the intangible reality of the dogmas and commandments required to preserve the Harmony willed by the Law of Creation created by the Eternal. The unique bond that keeps us so fragilely alive on this Earth will only subsist on this single but vital celestial condition.

"For God nourishes heaven with his radiance;
For Heaven in turn feeds the Twelve;
For the Twelve nourish the Divine Parcels;
Because the Parcelles are the gifts given to humanity.

"Fear, then, O all you who listen to me, always and forever, the renewal of the Almighty's wrath, for although mankind feeds on the bounties of food dispensed by God on Earth, He can take them away from them at any moment, in the space of a second, if wrath manifests itself against the impious!

"This is why, in the continuation of the beneficial cycles of the blessed Sep'ta loved by Heaven, those who deny or repudiate their belonging to the divine race may live in false abundance on Earth, but will be rejected in Heaven. They will remain the eternal reprobates when their bodies rot. They will never be able to reach our Elders, who nevertheless extend their spiritual influence to bring them to them. It is to avoid all future misunderstandings, as well as the possibility of misinterpretation through forgetfulness, that we must ensure a perfect understanding of the theology of our Fathers, transmitted and then brought back, at the cost of millions and millions of disappeared.

"As for all of you who are zealous servants of God, never doubt the supreme goodwill of granting us his manifold blessings. But it is not appropriate to seek, either in one's soul or in heaven, any testimony or sign of this certainty.

You are far better educated than the people, to know that the only valid and palpable sense of this beneficial action is that of which you have made yourselves the ardent defenders: the observance of the commandments stemming from Divine Law. Through its mathematical combinations, it has placed the Fixes far up in the sky so that their rays are multiplied by twelve before mixing with the Errants to form the essential basis of the 3,240 basic celestial configurations, the edicts that allow us, in the course of our various navigations, to calculate and define Man's time, his earthly life and his afterlife, according to the systematic order preconceived by God.

"Each of the priests that you are must teach this fundamental Truth, which there is no need to insist on here, as the reality of Mathematical Combinations is updated daily in front of us. Groups of four novices will accompany you from today, to help you in the supervision of the engravers charged with reproducing, on the lower wall sections assigned to them, the texts in sacred characters, those newly redefined since the cessation of service of our Divine Language. This will accustom the young novices to fix their attention on this calligraphy in our new written language.

"You must take scrupulous care to ensure that none of the workers changes the intended arrangement of the members of the sentences or inverts any of the characters. No drawing may be removed or added. No word is to be written in this way in the place of another so that the teaching bequeathed by the Elder remains as pure as it was on the first day.

"I say this solemnly to you all on this day, which brings us ever closer to the date of our union in a new covenant. For this new community to grow and multiply its branches rapidly into an indestructible bough, no one must innovate in any way in the observance of the divine commandments that have been handed down to us! Not even the seed of a sterile dispute should ever touch your minds, so that the precepts that your children's children will learn remain in their integrity without ever undergoing any alteration!

"May the peace of the Son of Usir, blessed be he, accompany you at every step. Amen!

With a muffled hubbub, the religious rose from their benches and respectfully bowed to the Pontiff, their leader. Without a word, they followed one another towards the small door of the hall, which seemed to open by itself, as if by magic. They emerged in a display of immaculate tunics.

Merit-Nout then stood up, beckoning his two assessors to do the same. Their footsteps echoed as they crossed the room, which had suddenly taken on its imposing dimensions. When they reached the hypostyle hall, the three clerics followed the central aisle alone towards the exit of the temple, whose two doors were wide open. Once again, the Pontiff was satisfied with this respectable construction, the result of plans by his venerated predecessor Meri-Hotep. Every detail was a reminder of the cult of the Ancients, which they should respect in their fidelity to divine tradition. The sanctuary reserved here for Hor symbolised his birth, by Usir, the son of Ptah, and Iset, daughter of Nut and Geb. The whole edifice was a song of glory for the Divine Triad, and this was indeed how God had wanted it.

On reaching the threshold, An-Nu stopped to contemplate the progress of work on the great temple, the one dedicated to Nut, the Lady of Heaven. The two priests accompanying him did the same.

The building now appeared in all its sacred fullness. Just by looking at it, any human could see that they had reached the original Holy of Holies, the primordiality of Ptah, Lord Almighty of Ta-Nout-Râ-Ptah!

The closer the monks got to it, following a gentle upward slope, the more the serene, peaceful smile of the Lady of Heaven Nut appeared to them in all its living fullness. The six pillars of the main entrance, circular but three times the diameter of a human being, were surmounted by a figure of the Virgin Queen, who had become the Protector of this Mecca for observing the sky and the combinations that abounded there. The imposing mass barely let in the light of the sun and when the Pontiff entered the hypostyle hall, followed by his two companions, Ra's rays played on the folds of the immaculate tunics, showing those who were silently walking around three white spots moving against a very dark background. An-Nu knew his way by heart. He could have walked with his eyes closed to the sunset opening that gave access to a staircase within the walls, with no windows to light it, and which led, after climbing one hundred and forty-four steps, to the upper terrace that served as an observatory and near which was the secret place: that of the warning sky map!

Once this climb had been completed, the Pontiff looked out from the small uncovered room, which was brilliantly illuminated in gold, and saw the workmen, divided into several groups and working together on scaffolding in the next room, engraving the ceiling according to the precise data of the sky on the day of the Great Cataclysm.

The inner circle, with its Twelve and Ptah as the great central Judge, was practically complete. The middle circle, with its calculating elements and the seven Wandering Women, was being polished on the eastern side, while the opposite side was also finished. Two specialised workers were artfully and lovingly polishing the large figure of Nut, her outstretched hands and toes touching the two side walls of this chamber. This chamber was thus the landmark of the Fixes of the third circle, but also the link uniting Earth and Heaven to protect all the descendants of her two sons: Osiris and Set, united in the same unique maternal love.

The engraving of the last circle had several teams to satisfy a fair representation of more complicated scenes. The aim was to depict the thirty-six diurnal elements that enabled the exact calculation of the catastrophe before it happened, and this was vital as proof of the value of Mathematical Combinations for the future of the chosen people.

Just where the new setting of the sun in Leo had occurred on the evening of the first day navigation in the other direction, an engraver was chiselling the silhouette of Geb, the last king of Ahâ-Men-Ptah, carrying on his head all the weight of the Earth, which he would bring back to life thanks to the understanding of divinity granted to Nut, his wife through the birth of Uzir.

The Masters of Measurement and Number, who had perfected this transmission of historical and spiritual data, had also made it easier to understand by implanting, just above the disc supported by Geb, a Lion who turned his head, opening his mouth and sticking out his tongue viciously. What's more, his front legs were firmly supported by the hieroglyphic sign of the cataclysm (eight vertical broken lines), which seemed to dominate him perfectly. Finally, Geb himself was girded with a lion's skin, its great tail touching the ground to symbolise the union, the link and the new harmony that would henceforth reign between heaven and earth.

Meri-nut smiled at the ingenuity of the key that would have made it possible to understand this series of thirty-six figurines, so important for combinatorial calculations. In fact, just in front of Geb's face was engraved the hieroglyphic of the two stars known today as alpha and beta of the Centaur, surmounted by the chick emerging from the sunken capital. It was the second multitude ready to take flight towards its second homeland: Ath-Kâ-Ptah.

The second drawing, as well as the third, on the left of the lower circle, were located under the feet of a chair with a lion's profile, on which Nut was sitting holding one of her two sons in her hands. But the Masters had intentionally left this face featureless, so that the reader could imagine it to be either Set or Usir, as he wished. But the two figures below are clearly drawn in the effigies of both. And while Set wears the horns of a ram, Usir, who also wears them, also wears his father's globe. Between the two brothers, the hieroglyph of annihilation. In front of Set's face, the two hieroglyphs that marked the day of the great cataclysm: the Lion's hindquarters and the earth balanced on an upturned sky. What's more, here too, the ancient mathematicians had correctly guessed the location of the engraving, since the stars of the Southern Cross were right between the two brothers, under the sign of annihilation.

Then come the figures symbolising the long exodus through the asterisms of the various Fixes leading to the colure of the solstices of the true North. There are four of them: Horus with the only crown of the Sleeping Blessed, then Isis, then Horus but with the chief of the two lands, the lost one and the one promised in the

New Alliance, perfectly defined with the spiral of Creation added to the double crown. Finally, the Elder, the Descendant, the one who will unite the two fratricidal clans. In addition to the lion's skin and tail dragging to the ground, he carries the mane. Above him, the Celestial Cow watches over the smooth running of earthly events.

Next comes the ibis-headed scribe, who will personify the person who will bring hieroglyphics back into use. He is the renovator of the sky and of the new generations. The new generations, always highlighted by Horus the Sparrowhawk, make a brief stop. The bird is the ninth character, reintroducing the Divine Word into everyday life. The star Canopus serves as a landmark.

An ideographic set, already perfectly drawn on the ceiling, is the subject of the tenth image. Another team is working on it. A parallelogram starts from the outside of the circle, on which a snake with the head of an ibis moves in four circles. This is, of course, the scribe teaching the multitude to obey the divine commandments. The Patriarch who walks above, clutching his sceptre, carries on his shoulder the sign personifying the star Orion, a landmark as important as Sirius for calculations.

The descendants of the two clans that follow them have no attributes on their skulls. They tirelessly continue their Exodus towards the East, and the fifteen five-pointed stars that count down the time provide the duration. And the pig that precedes them, head down, indicates that this troubled period must be, if not forgotten, at least relegated to a place beyond the reach of the new calendar.

And the despised offspring, depicted by a naked young woman kneeling with her hands on her thighs and three snakes emerging from her headdress, shows the arrival of God's usurpers: the worshippers of the sun, with the entry of the constellation Aries. She is depicted at on her celestial boat, just below her representation in the spiral of the Twelve.

In front of its head, four snakes with human heads crawl on another quadrangular block. The upturned knives of Set l'assassin above them show that they are the children of the deceitful and the envious, trying to take advantage of mathematical combinations that seem to be in their favour.

The child crouching on a blossoming lotus leaf, who precedes them, has a finger over his mouth to impose silence on those of his race who would rebel against this rebellion against Ptah. For what is written cannot be undone by the hand of man, and God does not seem to want to come to the aid of those who are certainly his creatures, but who increasingly doubt his reality. Nevertheless, the child wears on his shoulder the symbol of a plough for harvesting, proving that work can renew thought.

As this engraving is located on the cardinal point of the true east, the symbolism of the renewal of time is even more clearly understood.

The following Horus, with the head of a sparrowhawk, who walks next, wears three celestial symbols above his hair, which attract a great deal of attention. They are: a ram's head, a heart emerging from an urn, and an upside-down sky. Taken together, they clearly indicate a renewal foreseen by the astral configurations just as the Sun enters the constellation of Pisces, just above.

It is followed by an important symbol: a royal seat on which is placed a human form whose head cannot be seen and whose top is bound. It represents Uzir imprisoned in his bull's skin, ready to be resurrected. The Eye of Creation, in the circle above, demonstrates the renewal coming from an Elder for the second time at the solar entry into Pisces. A whole iconographic ensemble then follows, seemingly scattered, but linked by the same idea.

Six fledglings, in two groups of three, follow an expressionless human face, while two Aries heads, below, are embedded in granite blocks, immobilised to allow the children of God to take flight again. A sun casts nine rays over the scene, while a priest of Ptah, holding out his breastplate in front of him, uses it as an emblem to preach the monotheism that is taking flight. This is symbolised by the dove resting on the breastplate but stretching out its wings, ready to take flight.

Obviously, Set, in his representation of the ferocious jackal, does not appreciate this and tries to re-establish the primacy of the ram. Geb, again in his symbolism of the goose, is trying to prevent not only the battle, but the complete destruction of two offspring born of his wife and himself. The fourteen five-pointed stars that appear above Geb make it possible to calculate this space of time with the revolutions of the Fixes that appear there, in particular Formalhaut. And the Elder of the Elder-Heart, also drawn above the stars in the spiral of the Twelve, holds precisely the two urns that will pour water from the sluices of heaven if the Cadets of the Second-Heart continue to be blinded by their selfishness.

The large oval medallion, in the shape of what was later called a cartouche, which is engraved in the following location, features eight human figures kneeling with their hands tied behind their backs. This cartouche, starting from the beak of the goose Geb, seems to muzzle any desire on the part of the bird to oppose the march of time, imprisoning the Rebels of monotheism, the creator of Creation, without whom the sun itself would not exist. The Fixed Epsilon of Capricorn that surmounts it is indicative of the date.

The Elder with the head of an ibis who precedes him announces the formal resolution of the one who set the chronology of the chosen people in motion on the orders of the Almighty not to change anything more in the order established in the celestial mathematical combinations. Time is thus counted down, as if by a water klepsydra whose seconds flow irretrievably drop by drop.

Beneath the front legs of the Capricorn of the Twelve stands a priest in a long white tunic, but with the head of a hawk, which is unique in all this prophetic representation. He is an Elder who is also Pontiff of the Kingdom. What's more, a ram follows him, its head surmounted by the solar disc. So this Son of God is also the shepherd and guide of those who were rebels. He gives his hand to the figure before him, who has no face, his face being replaced by an empty circle. He is therefore the Divinity in person. A true Son who will give proof of what he is, demonstrating that he is the one we cannot see and whose true name cannot be pronounced.

Another human with the head of a hawk, this time wearing only the skin of a lion, gives his hand to another Elder wearing the double crown of the two countries of AhâMen-Ptah. They are under Sagittarius. But it is Set, with the head of a jackal, in front of them who, for the purposes of the calculations, is under the alpha and beta fixes of Sagittarius, while above, the Mandjit bearing Set's victorious Horus watches over the birth of another world.

What is commonly known as a typhoon silhouette follows this series of images. This one is a crouching hippopotamus, its face marked with a six-pointed star. A Mandjit protects it from the inevitable bad weather, so that it can serenely watch over the future delimited by the key of three five-pointed stars that it holds against its abdomen. The bow of his sacred boat is up against the altar bearing the head of a grimacing jackal: Set.

The circle is about to be completed, and the thirty-fourth figure is the much revered Usir. His body is symbolised as it was when he was imprisoned in the skin of a bull. In his cocooned appearance, he has not yet resurrected and is leaning against the altar dedicated to Set. The two attributes of his supreme kingship are in his hands. Not only will he seal the new covenant, but he will also send his descendants to populate the rest of the Earth.

The last two figures therefore set off towards the Sunset, each in the place prescribed to him, and depending on their good or bad divine management, this will be the end or a new beginning. The West, rediscovered after the thirty-sixth figure, is once again the Master of a new great year of almost twenty-six thousand years, or of a more or less serious disturbance of the world's axis.

An-Nu, the Pontiff of this new land, heaved a sigh. This magnificent planisphere in the form of a prophetic warning had led him far from his sole concern: the completion of the Golden Circle.

And on a much larger scale, this would also be the finger of God within the reach of the Wise, and the fear of all the wicked!

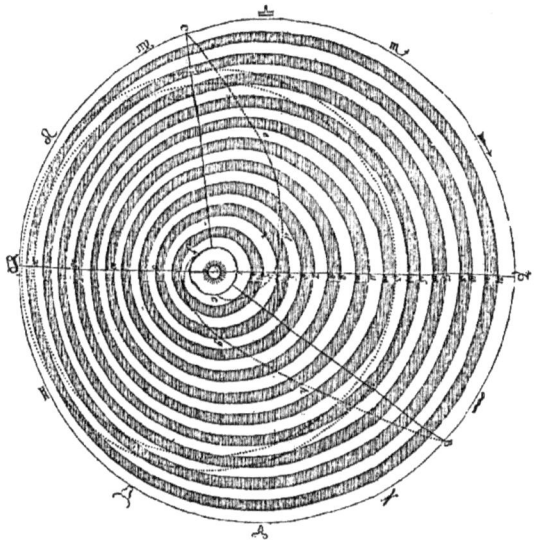

The Twelve encircle the earth in twelve off-centre influxes.
However, the calculations are easy and straightforward to reconstruct.

Chapter V

DIVINE MATHEMATICAL COMBINATIONS

> *"You shall plaster large stones with lime. Then you shall write on them all the words of this Law, so that you may enter the land given to you by your God, flowing with milk and honey, as the God of your fathers has said to you."*
> Old Testament
> *(Deuteronomy, XXVII --2/3.)*

> *"The holiness of this God says:*
> *Instruct him in the words of the past; they will be the food of children and of grown men. He who understands it will walk in satisfaction of heart. His word will never cause satiation.*
> Preamble to the Treaty of Ptah-Hotep
> *(Papyrus found by M. Prisse).*

"On this memorable day, the beginning of a new year dedicated to Ptah, our sole support throughout the millions of difficulties that have marked our path over the millennia, let us give thanks to him above all else. Glory to Ptah!

All the assembled students repeated these three words with unprecedented fervour: "Glory to Ptah!

The Master of Measurement and Number, Ank-Kâ-Hor[22], immediately undertook the first lesson in Divine Mathematical Combinations, thus linking up the ancient sacred tradition after a break of six millennia:

---

[22] "Living Breath of Horus."

- The Golden Circle is ready to receive you all, if you know how to prove yourselves worthy of the teachings you have learned from your various Masters. But from now on, know that the divine curse will irremediably follow in the footsteps of those who are too curious and who want to go further into the halls of the Double House of Life than they are allowed. You are aware of the various degrees involved in reading the Sacred Texts, for they include the study of the human sciences, followed by the understanding of Knowledge, which alone is capable of leading a human creature to the Divine Light. In this spiritual journey, it has been necessary to compartmentalise education into a number of initiatory stages to ensure that it is carried out safely. Man's "Divine part" must be spared, so that it can learn all that concerns it, without being disturbed. Truth can only be taught under certain obvious conditions. Therefore, the future "Masters of Measurement and Number" that you are, must begin their approach to Knowledge with only its simplest aspects, to avoid a too human inclination later encouraging them to complicate the Truth in one way or another! This is why you will each learn according to how quickly you understand: first the moral precepts, then the mathematical sciences and finally the Commandments of the Law with its Divine-Mathematical Combinations. This is possible today. For it was three hundred and sixty-five solar revolutions ago that the first work began. It was exactly a quarter of a year ago that the star of our good Lady Isis, blessed be she[23], sailed, that the venerable Pontiff, religious leader of the two clans finally unified, the Holy Bâ-En-Pou, undertook to finalise the plans for the Golden Circle on the site assigned to him by God, in his mercy towards us. This Patriarch, my direct ancestor, was the eldest 211[e] in the direct line from Anepou, who was the closest Apostle of Usir. So, in a quarter of a revolution of the brilliant Sep'ti[24], the most magnificent reproduction of all celestial mechanics and its thousands of cogs, the Divine-Mathematical Combinations, was assembled piece by piece. Today, it is at our disposal, so that the future will once again

---

[23] Sirius has a revolution of 1 461 years, i.e. 365 years 1/4 for a quarter revolution.

[24] Hieroglyphic name for Sirius.

conform to the past, if the human spirit, with its divine fragment, does not once again rebel against this universal harmonic reality which forms an indivisible whole, and which is here made palpable, alive and real to you. As if by the impulse of a gigantic cosmic clock, the Creator has modelled a meticulous and precise celestial machinery, whose mechanics cannot be regulated by God and can only be eternal, in relation to the Humanity engendered to benefit from the Nature placed at its disposal. But alas, at a certain point in the cycle that led to the proliferation of his environment, Man was no longer content to propose adjustments to Divine Law: he rejected the Image of the Creator that he is, to take himself for God! The result was the appalling catastrophe that we have all suffered the after-effects of for millennia and millennia, and which we want to erase forever from the Future for the New Covenant with God that we are in the process of signing.

A short break allowed the Master to ease the tense atmosphere. The minds of all the students were aware of the importance of this historical course, which would enable them to take back control of their own destinies. In front of each of them were sheets of papyrus and writing cases full of indelible ink, while a number of styles made from blunt ostrich feathers or pieces of reed cut into points were waiting to be used. Ank-Kâ-Hor, having consulted the freshly rewritten treatise before him, continued:

- Thus, since birth, humanity has retained its free choice between Good and Evil, each time disposing of its own misfortunes. It has retained the right to free will, walking towards the destiny it has forged for itself by accepting or denying this Divine Law, which has remained as immutable as ever in its pursuit of the Creation of the future. The Soul breathed into the beings of flesh that we are is quite rightly described as: "Divine Parcel". This is the impalpable but indissoluble link that binds every human body to the Creator. Whether those you will teach later admit it or not, the Truth is clearly defined in the crypt of birth:

"The carnal envelope that is moulded in the mother only takes on its human form when the bond that served as the root in the womb is separated. From that

moment, it becomes a living being because it is then impregnated with its Divine Parcel by the Breath emanating from the Twelve, and which is personal to it."

"As you are no longer unaware from your early years of study, the Golden Circle reproduces the movements of the Fixed Ones and the Wandering Ones in their separate movements of day and night. However, two zones of influence must be delimited for each, because the mathematical combinations of the Wanderers with Ra and our Earth depend to a great extent on the influence of the "Twelve Fixed Ones" that form the Heart of Ptah. We shall shortly ascend to the highest terrace of the great temple, in order to observe their location in Heaven. Then I will ask you to point them out to me on the planisphere engraved in the room adjoining this observatory. This first lesson will show you the usefulness of such a construction for preserving such knowledge. And when you reach the supreme degree of Knowledge, you will have counted 30 times 12 times 7 plus 30 times 12 times 2 chambers, i.e. 3,240 rooms with walls that move and change according to the Divine-Mathematical Combinations of day and night.

Ank-Kâ-Hor quickly flicked his sleeves, stretching out his two long arms towards the crowd of students before continuing with the subject he knew so well:

- From the moment of his birth, the human being is invested with the name of Man, and is fully responsible to the Creator. When he reaches the age to give himself the constitution of another carnal envelope likely to receive a new Divine Parcel, he must suffer the consequences of all his other humanitarian acts, especially when they are knowingly and deliberately committed to distort Divine Law. Man is incapable during his short time on earth, not even a second of eternity, of understanding the movements of the Cosmic Machine. It took thousands of years of patient, meticulous observation by the first 'Descendants of the Elder' to annotate, compare and define the commandments imposed by the universal rule, so that Man could live only in the Good, failing which he would perish from the Evil he would unleash himself! Complicated though they may appear, the gears that punctuate the various movements are well-oiled. Each fleeting moment of eternity determines the regular advance or retreat of the Suns, which are the hearts of the twelve celestial equatorial constellations. It makes them pulsate to form geometric configurations, which are the "Divine-Mathematical-Combinations". In their relationship with the "navigation" of our Sun along the banks of the Great Celestial River Hapy[25] we find all the keys to the predetermination of the permanent agreement between heaven and earth, which must be reflected in Harmony: the Alliance between the Creator and His Creatures. For Creation began millions of centuries ago! Ptah the one, in six different but mathematically fractionable periods of time, as you have already learned[26]. The seventh period began with that of the camel envelope which, receiving a Divine Particle, became Man. And this moment could not take place either before or after the predetermined day because the Belt of the Twelve Fixes was not in place beforehand to send us its influxes here below. Each of the Twelve Fixes being endowed with its own natural qualities, and using their radiations to bring them to a single centre: the Earth, humanity could only be born, grow and prosper in this ideally privileged place. If our souls were influenced solely by these mathematical combinations, there would be far too many kindred spirits. They would be jealous of each other, unable to get along or form alliances, and there would be perpetual struggles that would irrevocably lead to the annihilation of all human life. Divine mathematics has solved this problem by instituting innumerable variants that disrupt the radiation of the Twelve by that of the Wandering Ones of our system, which number seven. What's more, this system is further duplicated by the Moon's night-time modification of all the results obtained. We therefore have, within our grasp, a universal clock on a cosmic scale, each second of which determines the direction of a Divine Subdivision in its earthly life, according to one of the 3,240 primordial modes. You have been taught everything you need to know to find your way back, after each study in a part of the Golden Circle. This can only be valid on

---

[25] The Milky Way, on whose shores are the 12 zodiacal constellations.

[26] On this subject, read chapter 3 of The *Great Cataclysm*, devoted entirely to this creation.

the condition that you do not venture off the path mapped out daily for each of you. If you were to stray, no one would come to your aid. You would be condemned to perish from hunger and exhaustion, because you would be unable to find your way back, and no one would point it out to you! The layout of the rooms and corridors has been designed to make your task easier, but also to prevent you from wandering off into the world, which would inevitably end up at the bottom of a deep well... The sole aim of this Golden Circle is the purest transmission of Divine Knowledge and the transformation of Creation. These two primordial original principles, which have come down to us intact in the sunken East of our Elders, and which God, for our incessant reminder, has now located at the Sunset of our "Second Heart", but allowing us to recall that they knew the Law of Creation from the earliest days, when their Divine Parcel awoke. We must therefore relentlessly and tirelessly preserve its absolute integrity, so that our race, which was the Chosen One, may live again in all its splendour, of which we are merely the survivors on borrowed time. But the future "Pêr-Ahâ", our descendants of this Elder who was the first to teach us how to use a spirit, will soon begin the Great Cycle of the Renaissance, as predicted by the future "Mathematical Combinations". From now on, it is appropriate to leave to them the tracing of all the celestial configurations and their handling. These Annals, carved in stone indestructible by the wear and tear of time, and untouchable by men because of the place where they are engraved, will thus remain the surest guarantors of this Renewal of a Covenant with God. In this way, the flesh of our flesh will be educated according to the Divine Law and its Commandments for its greater good, so as to avoid a cataclysmic renewal, such as that which engulfed our "First Heart": Ahâ-Men-Ptah!

The Master of Measurement and Number took a deep breath, as if to put off the catastrophe for a very long time. He even forced himself to smile as he continued:

- In a few moments, the great feast of Sep'ti will begin with prayer in the great temple of Nut, the Good Lady of Heaven, in the presence not only of our venerated Pontiff, but also and above all with TêtaMéri, our Pêr-Ahâ, who arrived this morning from his distant northern capital. He will solemnly re-establish the calendar and the sequence of years, months, days, hours, minutes and seconds. Time will indeed regain its meaning. And we, for our part, will be ready to give it its full meaning. Before we go to the special prayer for this memorable day, I would just like to add this, which concerns the legitimacy of the Knowledge of the Divine-Mathematical Combinations, and thus the Knowledge of the Future. You are all already aware of the influence of the state of the sky on your daily behaviour, and of the virtues that can derive from it if you don't allow yourself to simply put up with it. The same is true of our entire environment, and it's essential to follow the seasons to sow vegetables or harvest fruit at the right time. Nature is subject only to seasonal changes, which we have to undergo because they are driven by celestial combinations. The Sun, barring a new wrath from God who remains the Almighty Master, is the geometrical element that will enable all the combinatorial calculations with the Wandering and the Fixed, for it is the Sun that ultimately gives Life to humans, animal generations and fertility to everything that breathes, fish and plants alike. Through its daily navigation, it warms, caresses, causes sap to rise, dries, burns and refreshes by causing the waters of the great river Hapy to rise, accomplishing all this in a mathematical order willed by the Creator to advance His Creation according to the rhythm set by the combinatorial palpitations. This obviously applies to all the days God gives us. But when the Sun sets in the West, above the Amenta, to give back to our Blessed Ancestors asleep in Ahâ-Men-Ptah the Life in the Celestial Fields, the black cloak of night spreads over our heads. The Moon then takes over from the Sun and sets the pace of Time according to its own navigation. Much closer to the Earth than the Sun, the Moon has a more direct influence on human beings, who feel the power of its movement as much as of its reflecting light. Because it acts like a mirror, its power is distorted. The Great River rises and falls with it every day, imitating its rising and setting. Plants and animals do the same, changing their nature according to the easily calculated angles of refraction. These effects are counteracted or strengthened by the radiations of the Twelve and the glances they have between them. The Knowledge of the Future is a vital element of Knowledge, but one that is oh so perilous. Only those who are able to discern in advance how to use it, and especially with whom, will be able to master it! For this disclosure is extremely dangerous, and that is why I must draw your attention to this problem. Under no circumstances should the lure of gain or power be the justification for your intervention to change anything in the future of a human being! Many ploughmen already only sow their fields according to precise beneficial conjunctures; many shepherds only allow their animals to mate according to strictly defined astral periods. So never allow yourself to predict the future for the pleasure of showing off your knowledge and winning adulation. There is only one god and he is God the One! Man is only man, and even the most ignorant of men is capable of predicting the weather and playing the magician! Indeed, the most remarkable influences with their most notable meanings, concerning the combinations of the Sun, the Moon and Sirius, to say the least, are so certain that observation alone has enabled anyone to notice them and to use them as a matter of course for those whom necessity leads to use them. So it is with the boatmen, who don't need our rising water indicators to know when the river is at its highest. On the other hand, they do have to watch out for winds and rain, the frequency of which is not obvious. They have to rely on certain lunar configurations conjoined with a wandering star, or a fixed star in quadrant with the Sun. And there, because of their ignorance, they have no absolute knowledge of the weather, only an approximation. And who would prevent an initiate, later on, from teaching these ignorant nautoniers the art and the manner of forecasting the weather and of knowing the locations of the wind shifts? Simply by not making him an Initiate, since the various degrees of passage to a higher grade are only accessible to those who have fully satisfied all the tests. To reveal even a small part of the Knowledge to an uninitiated human being is to make greed glow in his heart and leave the field open to this unprepared spirit to become caught up in a kind of madness by wanting to be equal to God! Only those of you who pass all the tests will know all the movements of time, the places assigned to the Twelve, the Sun and the Moon, in the present and in the future, in order to draw their links with each other at every hour of the day and night. As for the rest, which is no less important, you already know the mathematics of the system. Ever since God, in his anger, upset the solar navigation by making it grow from east to west, the revolution of this star has been going backwards for 25,920 years. This is the first point you have all studied. The second relates to Sep'ta, the star dedicated to Ptah, because on this earth, here very precisely, when it appears for the first time each year above the horizon delimited by the wall of the observatory on the highest terrace, it announces the start of the flooding of the Great River. It also determines all the solar calculations for a period of 1,461 years, since it is at the end of this period that a new year begins, thanks to an exceptional conjunction with the Sun. As you know, in a few hours' time Sep'ta will reappear, not only to herald the flooding of the river, but also in conjunction with the Sun, visible at exactly the same point just before sunrise. So this has been calculated for centuries and centuries, and everything has been designed to unfold as it will shortly. We are about to enter the first day of the first month of the year ONE of the new era of the Celestial Bull, the era that will ensure the supremacy of the younger people of Uzir for at least two millennia. I've finished for today: it's time to go to the Great Temple! Come on..."

Before turning to the son of the great Mena, the first Pêr-Ahâ of Ath-Kâ-Ptah, in the company of Ank-Kâ-Hor, it would be a good idea to place the precise moment of this historic scene in greater detail.

This precise day of renewal in the Gothic calendar (Spt'ta, or Sirius, is called Sothis in Greek) was 15 June 4244 BC in the Gregorian calendar, or 19 July of the same year in the Julian count, which is the one adopted here. You can be sure of the exact date, as there are many astronomical references to it. The latest is relatively close, dating from 139 AD. We owe it to the eminent historian Censorinus: "In the twelfth calendar of August, during the consulship of the emperor Antoninus Proessus, i.e. on the 20th of July in the year 139, there was the beginning of a great cycle, due to the conjunction of an Egyptian Thoth with the rising of the heatwave. We were thus approaching the hundredth completed year of the cycle of this heliacal, heat-wave year, also known as the "Year of God".

If the reader is to understand this vanished civilisation, it is essential to grasp its primordial need to live according to purely celestial and astronomical data, which in fact merged with the Divinity.

Now, since the Great Cataclysm, the Survivors were due to be reborn in a Second Heart, six millennia earlier. So when Mena completed the unification of the two fratricidal clans on the Second Earth, begun three centuries earlier by Nar-Mer, he knew that it would be his son Tê-Ptah who would reintroduce, when the time came, on the first day of a new year of God, writing, the calendar, medicine and all the elements needed to begin a new history made in the image of God's will.

Mena reigned for sixty-two years, driven by a fierce determination to achieve unification in an indestructible pact. For this reason, he founded the capital of the new state on the banks of the delta, not far from present-day Cairo, at Mennefer, which the Greeks turned into Memphis. It was there that he first had a magnificent temple built to thank Ptah the One, to which he gave the name Ath-Kâ-Ptah, the Second Heart of God. This name then became the real name of Mennefer, then under the son of Têta: Atêta (the Athothis II of the Greeks) the name of the whole country, replacing Ta Mérit (The Beloved Place, or the Promised Place).

During the last four years of his reign, Mêna took his son Têta in co-regency beside him, so as to allow him to immerse himself in the grandiose role that would be his. Having ruled in this way from 4307 to 4245, Mena died during a hunt, when an angry hippopotamus trampled and killed him.

From that moment on, Teta, or rather Tê-Ptah, alone held the Sceptre of the two clans, ready for the divine role that had been predestined for him from his capital at Mennefer. As we shall see later, Tetah remained the Ahâ, the Elder, the Son of God who restored the integrity of a single people. Greek legend turned this Teta into Theot, half-scribe, half-God of Hellenic mythology, transforming him into Mercury. For the same reason, Ahâ Têta became Athothis, and again Thot for the first month of the calendar.

But it was time to rejoin Ank-Kâ-Hor who, having left the classroom, was about to climb, followed by his pupils, the inclined plane above the vast esplanade giving access to the Temple of the Lady of Heaven, enclosed by a high, very wide surrounding wall made of baked bricks and mortar mixed with river silt. Below them, the immense courtyard was filled with people from all over the country who had come to witness this grandiose and solemn opening of the passage of time.

Halfway up the slope, on a landing, stood a makeshift altar, one of dozens scattered here and there, surrounded by a wide walkway crowded with people eager to place their offerings to God in the many banded jars set out for the purpose. The gifts were intended not only to obtain the remission of many sins but also to obtain the second covenant so necessary for the renewal of this second earth. And the mountains of gifts of all kinds showed, in the very face of the Creator, the desire of his creatures to begin this year of God under the most favourable auspices.

Ank-Kâ-Hor walked slowly up the path until he reached the entrance to the great hypostyle hall, where the huge crowd of worshippers had gathered from all over, from the far south, where the believers were black of skin, to the mouth of the Great River, where men, women and children had blue eyes. Not only would all these people only see such a New Year's Eve celebration once in their lives, but their children and their children's great-grandchildren would only be able to re-read all the twists and turns of this fantastic event, because the commemoration would only take place in 1,461 solar revolutions!

With its twenty-four pillars measuring almost two metres in diameter and twenty-four cubits high (around thirteen metres), supporting a blue ceiling dotted with golden stars, the ensemble was imposing in both its size and its structure.

With the massive door of the Sanctuary still closed, the Master of Measurement and Number realised that the Pêr- Ahâ Têta was still locked up in the Holy of Holies in the company of the Pontiff and the high priests in order to meditate in front of the Mandjit, which according to Tradition was the one that transported Iset to the shores of Ta Mana. The building was made of solid stone with no openings. It was a Naos of meditation, where no one would dare venture, or even cast a single glance, on pain of appalling punishment, unless they were of divine essence, i.e. the Elder himself, the Pontiff, or the initiated High Priests.

Hank-Kâ-Hor sighed deeply, for from his studies he knew that in fact the sacred unsinkable boat contained in the room was nothing more than a faithful reproduction of the one that had saved the Good Lady of Heaven from disaster, and thus enabled the Survivors to live a second life! What was true, however, was that a piece of the real hull had been incorporated and preserved in the square base that supported it, and the bitumen covering it still smelt, at times, of Ahâ-Men-Ptah, as well as the horrors of the terrible catastrophe!

The gate opened at last, announced by the sound of drums and sistres. Soon there was silence. The Ahâ Têta appeared first, his face caught in the dazzling sunlight coming through an opening at the top of one of the walls. The Elder was still quite young, but his expression seemed unreal and imbued with an undeniable grandeur, as if he were living another life where age meant nothing. The Pontiff UsirKa left in his turn, followed by the College of thirty-four High Priests of Ath-Ka-Ptah. They had all come for this exceptional occasion, which concerned them. They formed a semi-circle around the Ahâ and the Pontiff, while the latter, raising both hands towards the countless smiling figures of Isis that adorned the tops of the pillars, spoke in a voice that was astonishingly clear and strong:

- O you, Iset, our good Lady of Heaven, this glorious day is yours! It only came about because your self-sacrifice for the survivors made it possible. Let it be the first of millions and millions of days. May this temple dedicated to you, O Nut, may your name be blessed for ever, be recognised until the end of time as the supreme refuge of the Twelve Breaths of the Divine Belt, may its Golden Circle be the Double House of Life, receptacle of the Celestial-Mathematical-Combinations. May the Pêr-Ahâ Têta, Elder Son of this Second Heart-of-God, direct descendant of Hor and of the Light of Ra, take charge of our destiny. Through this solemn meeting, we all pray to him here with the beating of our hearts united in a single vow, to bring the soul of this second earth back to life, by making effective once again the official institutions planned seal our second Covenant with the Eternal our God. In this way, the Twelve Breaths will bring harmony to all things and living beings on Earth, as well as in the Amenta and in Heaven. O you, Têta, Living Son of Ptah on Earth, I give you the second Sceptre of the government of Ath-Kâ-Ptah. You are Horus, the still living son of Osiris and Isis, who is thus placed on the golden throne of our Ancestors. Among them is Geb, the last king of Ahâ-Men-Ptah, who gave birth to Set, the "son of the Sun". Through him you also bear the envied title of Ahâ, "Beloved of the Sun". To this double divine title, you will add the one that will make you from now on and for all eternity: the Living Lord of Destiny.

Usir-Ka bowed his chest in deference, putting his immaculate white hair up to the belt made from a lion's tail, which closed the purple tunic of the Pêr-Ahâ. Têta kept his face as still as a statue, merely raising his right arm holding the Sceptre to indicate to the Pontiff that he should stand up. He then spoke in his very young, youthful voice:

- Hail to you, my father Usir, Lord of the length of time, Son of Ptah the One, whose many names, mysterious forms and transformations from beyond the earthly life inspire fear and respect in all mortals. From him, from his Celestial River, comes the water that feeds our Great River[27] ; from him comes the wind

---

[27] To make this vital speech by the Greek Athothis easier to understand, it has been translated into French. And what would seem normal in hieroglyphic would be less so here. Like the term HAPY, which meant both the celestial Milky Way and the terrestrial Nile.

and the breathable air; from him come the Twelve Breaths that impregnate us with the Divine Parcel when we are born. For in the days when Ptah, the Celestial Father, reigned alone over his Creation, he used his Word to transmit his vital force to the Twelve. This Divine Number, Master of Combinations, has impregnated, imprinted, fashioned and combined millions and millions of essentially different Divine Parcels, in order to breathe them, according to its sole combinatory will, into human carnal envelopes. The Twelve Breaths of the Celestial Belt thus follow a rigorous rhythm thanks to solar navigation divided into twelve monthly parts, and this for Eternity or the Time decreed by God. For the Twelve form the beginning and the end, good and evil, up and down, time and space, east and west, north and south. For the Twelve have an earthly beginning fixed from the beginning of time and its beginning in space for every moment of eternity, like life that is continually reborn from its dust. For the Twelve have an earthly end which is not an end, but an eternal renewal during the unlimited and mathematical cycles of the Years of Sep'Ptah, whose pulsations are set to the rhythm of the Celestial Combinations. For the Twelve showed the Harmony necessary for all life on Earth, allowing the unlimited: the thought of the soul, to enter the limited of the human voice. For finally, the Twelve, through the Commandments they specify, introduce the notion of justice. They are the implacable scourge of the Law of Creation. They form the balance between the plates of the Scales, advocating Good and denouncing Evil. This is why all the Pêr-Ahâ who preceded me waited for the Twelve to come to an end before raising the "Second Heart", our second homeland, from the ashes, so that life could resume here, just as it had stopped in Ahâ-Men-Ptah, our Elder Heart.

    The Ahâ Têta paused for a moment, overcome by a sudden emotion which he quickly tried to control. Then he resumed in total silence:

    This moment, so long awaited, so hoped for, so prayed for by all the Survivors, has arrived! I solemnly declare, in the name of us all, the first day of the first year of God of this Second Heart of Ptah, which has already begun. Glory to Ptah!...

"Glory be to Ptah! Glory to Ptah! Glory to Ptah!"

All the voices had shouted this triple vivat from the same heart. Many of the faithful were weeping. The emotion was intense, and the Pontiff Ousir-Kâ was also so moved that he almost forgot the protocol that obliged him to make an urgent announcement:

- Glory to Ptah! Glory to the Divine Triad! Glory to Ahâ Téta, Lord of Time on a par with Usir!

A short silence allowed the crowd to recover and fall silent in order to listen to the words of the An-Nu:

- For a few moments now, the seconds have been ticking away and the minutes have been ticking away. Our Scribes are already at work with their pens to record this memorable session. It is now time to give a name to each month of the solar year that will punctuate our daily time. The College of High Priests of the Second Heart has unanimously decided to name the first of the twelve months Teta, to honour forever the Ahâ who renewed our calendar. So today we enter the first day of the month of Teta. Long live Teta! Long live Teta! Long live Teta[28]!

Here too, there was only a huge cry in favour of the Eldest descendant of Horus. The Pontiff raised both his arms to show that he still had something to say, and once again there was silence:

- In order to solemnly close the pledge of our allegiance to the Commandments of God from this second onwards, Ahâ Têta, the Living incarnation of Ptah on Earth through Hor, from whom he is the direct descendant, will swear an oath to his Father before you all.

---

[28] As Ahâ Têta became Athothis in Greek phonetics, the month of Têta became, of course, the month of Thot, leading over the millennia to the legend of the god Mercury-Thot, patron saint of writers and writing!

For the second time, Usir-Ka bowed respectfully. As he rose, he joined the thirty-two High Priests who had raised their arms above the head of the Ahâ.

And so, Teta was able to complete this grandiose ceremony with a loud, proud voice:

- I solemnly swear, in the face of all the Cadets, not to interpose or change, in the order willed by Divine Harmony, a day, a month or a year. I solemnly swear to respect and not to modify in any way whatsoever any of the traditional religious festivals. I solemnly swear to observe the course of the 365 as it has been in the Elder Heart from time immemorial, rendered by the College of High Priests, the Grand Masters of Measurement and Number, under the high authority of the Pontiff, Master of the Double House of Life of the Divine-Mathematical Combinations.[29]

---

[29] This part of the oath taken by Teta in 4244 BC was always taken by the Pêr-Ahâ (Pharaohs) of the following thirty dynasties! It has been recorded in numerous texts, including by Nigidus Figulus, in the first century AD, in his Latin translation of the *Commentaries of Aratus*.

Chapter VI

THE FEAR

> "*In some cases, the hieroglyphic group Two Earths has heaven and earth as a variant. There often seems to be an intended ambiguity when the Egyptians speak of it, citing two opposite parts of the Universe.*"
>
> A. Moret
> *(On the religious character of the ancient Egyptians).*

> "*I have seen under the sun ungodliness in the place of judgement and iniquity in the place of justice.*
> *And I said in my heart: - God will judge the just and the unjust; then will be the time of all things.*"
>
> Old Testament
> *(Ecclesiastes chap. 3 - 16/17.)*

"So that you may always bear in mind the warning engraved on the map of the sky indicating the day of the Great Cataclysm, we shall all wear from that day onwards, at the top of the left sleeve of our High Priestly tunic, a special character, which will eternally be a reminder of the fear in a new wrath of Ptah against his Creatures."

The Pontiff heaved a deep sigh! Eleven solar revolutions had passed in the past since Ahâ Têta inaugurated the Golden Circle, but it seemed like centuries to him! His hair had barely turned white, but that famous fear of God's wrath had gripped him and oppressed him so much that he was still bent over. You could see it in his gestures and feel it in the more impersonal tone he used. In fact, the venerable Usir-Ka, despite being the greatest Initiate, had for eleven years been going through trials that were spiritually unprecedented and so evil that he had feared the total annihilation of the unified harmony achieved barely a century before.

What had happened? Ahâ Têta, who lived in his capital of Ath Kâ-Ptah, formerly Mennefer, or Memphis in its Greek phonetisation, near present-day Cairo, had obviously attracted envy and jealousy from the priests of Heliopolis who, while promising to observe the monotheism of Ptah, sacrificed to Ra. These priests, who were raising a descendant of Set, the "Worshipper of the Sun", in hatred of the Elder Teta, who they believed usurped the Sceptre, had him admitted as a prince counsellor of the double crown. And so it happened: Teta was assassinated by rebel conspirators from the Sun. But the usurper only held the reins of power for sixteen months: Teta's son, raised in the teachings of Ptah at Ta Nout-Râ Ptah, had escaped the massacre of his father and his family. It took the eldest son, Ateta (Athothis II of the Greeks), more than a year to kill, in a long and merciless battle, not only the traitor to the alliance signed by his fathers, but also the treacherous priests of An-Ra (Helio polis).

Ath-Kâ-Ptah, the Second Heart of God, had just shaken on its still fragile foundations. It was time, while retaining the fear of God, to act inexorably against those who transgressed any of his commandments. For Usir-Ka did not want to relive such a nightmare, and it would never happen again!

As he was going to give his youngest daughter as a wife to Pêr-Ahâ, it would be easier for him to direct his son-in-law towards a more severe policy towards any other impious religion. Hen-Nek, his favourite, so pretty and so intelligent, would help him greatly in this after her establishment as Queen-Divine. All the more so as she seemed to possess the remarkable gifts of the ancestor whose sacred patronymic she bore: Nek-Bet (the Nephthys of the Greeks).

The prospect brought him to his senses and he looked up at the novice priests who were patiently waiting for him to resume his lesson introducing the mathematical combinations inscribed in the Golden Circle. In a loud voice, Usir-kâ resumed:

- The new Pêr-Ahâ is due to pay us a visit soon. As the oldest of you will remember, Atêta was extremely kind to us all. We enjoyed a friendship in keeping with tradition, and he recently expressed a desire to make Hen-Nek his wife, which my beloved youngest daughter accepted with great pleasure.

A smile of connivance split the Pontiff's mouth, and the priests smiled in whispers of delight at the news, which was already circulating among them, but which now found its official confirmation. There would be great festivities in store!

Usir-Ka continued more seriously:

- We must therefore very quickly designate the teachers for each degree of initiation into the understanding of the Golden Circle, so that the Double House of Life which has just taken up its duties can send its most gifted students there without any problem. We must be ready to show the Pêr-Ahâ all the facilities that he did not know as a student, but which he should now see in every detail as Grand Master of the Universe, and therefore also of the Golden Circle. We need to standardise the probationary prologue to entry into the small classes of combinatorial movement studies. And we're going to start with this last question, as the other two can be resolved between yourselves.

With his long, nimble fingers, the Pontiff unrolled a few sheets of papyrus to remind himself of the main subjects to be dealt with, and how to highlight them later. Then, with a deep breath, he began:

- In the Beginning, the Impalpable, the Invisible, Ptah the Eternal created the Universe. He was then the only one truly alive. He created everything, and he alone was not made. Ptah exists from all eternity by his will alone, for he alone was not begotten. As Creator, he made heaven and earth as you have already learned. He is the Almighty Master of beings and non-beings, of all carnal envelopes and of course of all Divine Parcels. As for man, who comes from Him, he was created in the image of God to live in the divine way, according to His Commandments and in harmony with His Law of Creation. This is just a quick reminder of the teaching that we have all received, and which goes back beyond the successive transmissions made by our Elders, to the Son of Ptah himself. There is no doubt about it, for it is the expression of Truth itself.

With an almost imperceptible frown on his bushy, grizzled face, UsirKa picked up a palm wand from the table next to the papyrus and continued:

- Our Horoscopes have recounted Time from eleven solar revolutions, as it was practised more than fifty centuries ago, towards the current sunset, in our beloved First Heart, which has now disappeared. With this pointing instrument with a rear sight, it's easy to count down the hours. As soon as our sand clepsydras are perfected, real hearts will be beating to calculate the exact astral movements. This will not last long now, but in any case, the difference is so minimal in the operations to be carried out to draw the geometrical combinations of divine mathematics, that it is of no practical importance to us. Therefore, the following considerations will enable us to see in greater detail the great art of prediction offered by the study of the movements of the Fixed and Wandering of our sky. I have never been so convinced of the validity of predictions from the stars as I have been in recent years. All our prophets had a perfect knowledge of the celestial combinatorial movements, hence the announcements as valid as those predicting future catastrophes issued by our Ancestors. And if our venerated Ahâ Têta, who died so horribly, cowardly murdered by impious conspirators, had been willing to seek protection at the right time, as he had been advised, he would certainly be alive today. But as a Son of Ptah, he did not see fit to thwart the designs of heaven, for fear of upsetting a harmony that was already so precarious, by opposing this judgment of the stars. Grateful to him for this lofty spiritual thought, she plunged into deep reflection.

The An-Nu put down the palm wand which seemed to be in the way of his oratory, then continued:

- First of all, the Masters of Measurement and Number that you already are, or that you will soon be, must never worry in their way of warning or predicting about popular reactions. These will always tend to be mockery, envy and jealousy, for the Combinations and their solutions will be beyond the average understanding of the people. And if the prediction or prophecy comes true, there is a good chance that the public rumour mill of the ungodly will turn it into a chance encounter with reality! Never, therefore, deviate from the science of your art, which, through its natural causes due to divine mathematics alone, will ensure the long-term survival of your profession. The vanity of those who vainly try to imitate you for profit will then appear in all its sadness, and will thus be quickly detected and condemned. So that there is not, some day in the future, some injustice in this regard, you must, from today, keep the great secrets of this Knowledge safe from the usurpers of power and the wicked who have spawned these accursed worshippers of the sun! Besides, given the simplistic weakness of their souls, these humans will soon destroy themselves through their lack of knowledge of the greatness of this so complicated art. For you must understand that in addition to perfect calculation and skilful conjecture of the absolutely vital moving geometrical designs, this science of the attributes of God requires total harmonisation of the Divine Parcel with its Creator. Our commandments have their roots in the very essence of Creation, and the doctrine re-established with the new Golden Circle is a sure consequence of this. All the ancient configurations of the Fixed and Wandering created in Ahâ-Men-Ptah twelve millennia ago will find their exact reproduction in approximately the same period of time[30]. After such a long time span, the human mind alone is not sufficient to interpret the combinatory effects between them. And yet, Divine Mathematics amply demonstrates them, for they will meet on the desired day, conforming in every respect, everywhere they were expected. Since the examples are always identical, it is impossible for your predictions to be marred by errors or omissions. The only difficulty, and a perilous one at that, will lie in your interpretative judgement of the astral combinatorial phenomena you detect. So you will have to make a point of involving your conception of a future event as little as possible, in order to let your Parcel become impregnated with the only real cause of the movement of the celestial bodies in question. Where this will be even more exacting

---

[30] The Earth's precessional revolution is 25,920 years.

is in the judgements you will be called upon to make on certain human birth themes!

With a frank smile, Usir-Kâ recalled certain aspects of his personal studies, such as those of his youngest daughter and the current Pêr-Ahâ, and in a flash saw the propitious moment for a union that could not fail to take place! He straightened up a little more before continuing:

- The temperaments of each person, influenced since they took possession of them by the emissions of the Twelve in the irradiated form of a Divine Parcel, evolve as the solar revolutions unfold. Ra, as the directing arm of God's supreme will, deserves your full attention. I say attention, not veneration or adoration. All the combinations of the Fixed and the Wandering, at every second, unite with the Sun to produce the ordinary and particular qualities of each human being, and to make them evolve at every moment according to their own specific steps. For the diversity of the rays produced by all the 3,240 primordial Combinations clearly shows God's creative omnipotence in generating each thing at the time it was intended. It is so predominant, by its eternal conception, that it allows in the same second and in the same place to engender as many carnal envelopes desired by as many Divine Parcels preconceived differently. From this diversity alone, made possible by the Mathematical Combinations of the Twelve of the Law of Creation, comes the difference between the millions of human souls, even though the seed emitted by each man is essentially identical. The greatest power therefore resides in the only valid element, even though it is impossible to achieve on our earthly scale: the layout of heaven as willed by God from the depths of his eternity. This alone links us to the Eternal Creator, who enables us to see the reality of future problems, to predict them, and then to borrow from the combinations that detect them the beneficial principles that will be likely to modify and eliminate their malefic aspects. In this way, the meanings of celestial movements, even those that no longer depend on the configurations but on the personal suppositions that arise from them, will take on their full value. And since things are in line with the history of our good people and their still distant future, nothing will deceive you in your predictions. In this way, our Divine Science of Knowledge will forever be beyond reproach. Your great wisdom will preserve you for eternity as a leader of men!

Satisfied with this oratorical flight of fancy, the Pontiff drew a breath as he pulled up the sleeves of his tunic. The heat was taking hold of the entire atmosphere, and the air ducts were no longer providing the pleasant morning draughts. So Usir-Kâ hastened to resume, the silence having remained total in the midst of intense general attention:

- And if, one day or another, Ptah inadvertently no longer inspires you in the same benevolent way in your art, do not feel rejected or cursed by Him for some unacceptable reason; should the chiefs of the barges that transport our enormous blocks of stone and which, as a result of some unpredictable manoeuvre, sink to the bottom of the Great River, be made responsible for this? Of course not, and their future efforts will give rise to values a thousand times greater. The human spirit, the human soul, the Divine Parcel, which unconsciously knows its future from birth, must not seek to know more for the sole pleasure of knowing more, but to live better with its loved ones and its neighbours, to be enriched by it. The soul will be better suited to a beneficial community life. And just as it is impossible to condemn the doctors who are able to preserve intact for their time on earth certain carnal envelopes that are more perishable than others, those who have deserved to preserve a Divine Parcel from certain actions that are contrary to God's designs and who have not succeeded in doing so will not be held in contempt. This concludes my preliminary statement, which may be a little long, but which was necessary in order to penetrate more deeply into the Divine-Mathematical Combinations of our Golden Circle, as well as the predictions that can be drawn from the movements:t of the nature of the stars. Let us go beyond the acts occurring in the universe to concern ourselves only with the actions predefined for man and which derive from them by their causes. First of all, with the help of principles that are natural to man, such as his faculties for perceiving the waves of the Twelve, that is to say the radiation influencing the actions of the carnal soul on the length or brevity of earthly life. It is extremely useful to define this point perfectly in order to be its absolute master. For the purpose of man is not his earthly well-being, but the betterment of his spirit, since it will live forever. Indeed, what could be more gratifying for a being than to feel assured, if he observes the established rules, of rest and enjoyment in eternity? Ptah has taught us the rightness and justice of this doctrinal dogma. You will thus be able to teach better than anyone else what belongs to each Parcel in its own right, and what it is appropriate to attribute to it as a complement for the constitution of a personal temperament, capable of realising the beneficial influences pre-established for its sole intention. What will require your constant attention, through your fruitful directives, will be to put man on a path that could lead him to an increase in his earthly riches or too sudden an increase in his administrative burdens that could lead him to take himself for more than he is defined in the Combinations. As for all the enemies of our Faith, or all those envious of our prosperity and peaceful life, or all the opponents in general who will cry out to all winds of the falsity or uselessness of your work, it will be in pure loss, because it will be easy for you to prove their bad faith in the matter. They will only be driven to it by a dogmatic necessity: to prevent the prediction of their misdeeds and their superfluous undertakings with a view to bringing down the supremacy of God and His Creatures over the worship of idols and their rebels! It is quite true that these impious people prefer to remain in total ignorance of celestial influences, and even of those of Ra, their principal idolatry, so that they are only aware of their accidents when they occur, and then suffer them without being in a position to prevent them or to grieve over them if they are not the main victims. They prefer to say that a hazardous fate is the cause, and rely on what they call providence!

Raising his arms, Usir-Ka seemed to take heaven as witness to the futility of such an aberrant proposal, and with a deep sigh he continued in a less resigned voice:

- Our many millennia of foresight of all future events has accustomed our minds to govern themselves strictly within the precise limits God intended, so that today the soul is strengthened against foreseeable bad events in the future, as if they were close to us. This is made possible by your accurate forecasts, which prepare us to accept or change the things that happen to human beings through heavenly causes, which are in fact God's decrees, the decrees of fate, not immutable by the Law that created them, but transformable thanks to the covenant made between the Creator and his Creatures. No obstacle, not even the greatest, can be opposed as an imposition of absolute necessity to the free choice of the Divine Parcels to return, in all humility, to the perhaps narrow but necessary path that it will have left for a time to stray onto a road that is too adventurous. And while it remains constant that man's inferior actions change the pre-established order through disorder of some kind, even though they take the primary causes of their changes from heaven itself, the freedom acquired in earthly life makes it possible to re-establish total harmony before the imbalance has upset any attempt to re-establish order. Moreover, the very fact of this earthly freedom means that many unforeseen phenomena occur because of man's general bodily constitution, with all its complications and interweavings, and not because of his natural actions alone. But here too, fatal necessity cannot be called into question. The temperament of every being must evolve in the right direction, since it is obviously recognised from birth by characteristic data. The same applies to everything that is the object of the Almighty's celestial attentions, whose natural causes and principles receive the influences of the Twelve: minerals, plants, animals and all living things in general. From all their illnesses, all their discomforts, to which they are subjected by a certain necessity, the remedies of our doctors must cure them. Never forget that everything is in the One that is Ptah. The part of the whole that concerns our carnal envelopes is obviously the Belt of the Twelve, i.e. the central celestial zone that imprisons our Sun, the seven Errants and our Earth with twelve stellar groups practically linked to each other in a wide belt, hence the name imagined by our Ancestors, and fully justified. In order to impress upon our minds the truth of divine influxes, our first Elder, blessed be he, said that each of the twelve constellations possessed a gigantic, terrible heart, beating to the rhythm of the universe, and therefore of Ptah himself. It is these Twelve that God uses to send to Earth the infinite number of Parcels that populate, second after second, all the new carnal envelopes. In order to facilitate the study of the Divine-Mathematical Combinations, to make them comprehensible and to be able to retain easily all the terms of this celestial mechanism in perpetual motion, the first Masters of Measurement and Number, those who had in their minds alone all the data of the Universe, writing not yet having been established in their time, had to find names and images that were easy to locate. Thus, on the first day of their arrival on this earth, when they named it Ta Mérit: the Promised Place, they saw the sign of God's promise to them in the fact that the Great River, at night, was illuminated by the milky whiteness of the heavenly River that dominated it, and which appeared just as long and just as wide. Hence the name Hapy, a contraction of Ahâ and Ptah, made concrete by the phonetisation of the last letter. Hapy was therefore the patronymic used to thank the Elder Son, Usir, for his double benefit: the celestial sign and the earthly water. Our first Masters having rightly decided to locate the site of the Golden Circle here, as well as the Temple of the Lady of Heaven, it was obvious that the generic name of this celestial river, which had drawn all the Twelve to its banks, had to be that of Uzir's protector, the one who had given birth to him: the Virgin Queen Nut, blessed be she. And the Son having become the Celestial Bull, his mother became the Celestial Cow, Mistress of the Twelve.

One of the countless representations of the Celestial Cow, the Twelve attached to it and the obvious symbolism that follows.

Moved by this reminder of a bygone past that he certainly understood better than anyone else, Usir-Ka knocked several times on the pile of papyri spread out in front of him, to give himself composure before continuing his talk:

- For above Ahâ-Men-Ptah, whose outlines are no longer recorded in any of the documents in my possession, this celestial river was already nourishing the nights of our ancestors! And the Wandering Ones, who served as mirrors for the Twelve, had the same functions as today, but under the names they had before the horrible nightmare! Our Masters wanted to symbolise each of them by a second name, so as to bring to life Horus' last wanderings in search of his father, and then his revenge against Set. Thus, the Wanderer closest to Ra is called today, as you all know: Hor-Sep-Ptah. In those distant days, her mathematical combinations protected Horus from all the misdeeds of his uncle Set, and as on the day of his death she entered into conjunction with Sep-Ptah, this name has stuck to her[31]. Next in the order of the great circle comes the East Wanderer: Hor-Hen-Nut, and she typifies the grandmother's love for her grandson, a love that went as far as the greatest sacrifice ever recounted in our Annals[32]. Then there is the Red Wanderer, whom we still admire in her scarlet beauty: this is Hor-Py-Tesch[33], or Horus the Bloody. What better name to personify in eternity this son with a sunken right eye and a bloody left eye, a fractured right shoulder and a broken left knee, who nevertheless finds his father and saves him from annihilation so that he can rise again! After our globe, there are two more Wanderers: Hor-Cheta and Hor-Sar-Kher[34]. The first implies the Renaissance,

---

[31] It's Mercury, because the Greeks later called him Thoth the Scribe

[32] It's Venus, who has remained the goddess of love

[33] It's Mars

[34] These are Jupiter and Saturn

because its extremely beneficial position after the Great Cataclysm helped to bring about a favourable change in the lives of the Survivors descended from Uzir, while the other always influenced the outcome of the battles between the two fratricidal clans in the opposite direction. You often see the map of the sky engraved on the highest piece of the upper terrace,, with your pupils, and the position of these Wandering Ones on the spiral in relation to the figure of Ptah, leaning on the knife of Set the assassin, is striking enough not to return to it. But the entire march of the survivors is so well described and explained that it is a constant reminder of the setbacks suffered by the pioneers who were our Ancestors and Elders. And Nut, who covers this astral figure with her entire body, is its undisputed protector.

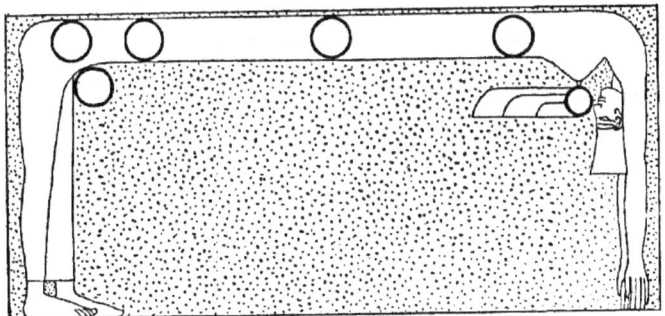

The Virgin Queen Nut always covers the azure encompassing our Earth. She gives birth to the new multitude and nurses them.

"May the blessing of Nut be perpetuated on us all!" mused Usir-Ka, catching his breath a little. The approaching times, which he had carefully studied since he was certain of the union of the young Pêr-Ahâ with his youngest daughter, left him no rest. His worries could only increase if what he had calculated from the astral combinations proved to be right! And why wouldn't they? It was better not to dwell on this data any further, since the two young people were not yet married! So the Pontiff continued briskly:

- What unlikely legends and tales will be invented in the generations to come! If we see what has already become of our ancestral History after six millennia spent among the people, it is difficult to imagine what will remain of our original heritage, and even more simply of the theology introduced by the Son himself, in another six thousand years. This is why every effort must be made, both in the narration of the lives of our Elders of the Amenta and in the education of the Cadets, to ensure that our chronology and our annals are transmitted in their entirety. One example is the Eye, whose six hieroglyphic parts symbolise the periods of Creation. This was our fundamental representation in Ahâ-Men-Ptah, because its very form made it possible to understand that this was the Creation[35], that carried out by the unique eye of the Eternal, the only "Great Seer" capable of creating such a great work as. Then, at the end of the Elder Heart, Usir was symbolically grafted onto this representation by his resurrection, becoming through this drawing "the Eye capable of looking its Father in the face". And finally, closer to home, Horus, having performed miracles with only one valid eye, was considered to be the first Redeemed by God, who had enabled him to perform miracles in this way. As a result, the Eye, which was originally intended solely advocate the various creative stages, became the property of the "Guardian of the Sleeping". Unfortunately, this is just one of the many examples where our tradition dating back to the beginning of the creation of the world places us today. We must do everything we can to re-establish the whole truth and to ensure that it does not deteriorate with time. To conclude this long preliminary, we must promise eternal happiness and complete satisfaction in this world to those who will totally follow the precepts that you will inculcate in them. For yourself and your pupils, never doubt that wisdom and science must go hand in hand in order to ward off the disastrous effects of the doctrine of the sun worshippers! You must act like a father towards his sons, and with all the authority with which he is impartial. Let your pupils become men in every sense of the word, created in the image of God, that is to say, men who must remain docile and cautious about everything that can be done against their future penetration into the eternal kingdom. Let this fear live in him, along with every beat of his heart. For this notion of the heart,

---

[35] A full description of this Creation can be found in *Le Grand cataclysme*, by the same author, published by Omnia Veritas.

whose double is the soul, must remind him of the end of the Elder Heart, his motherland, because the latter was no more than a prey given over to the impious and no longer to the Creators of God! The fear of God! It must live in us, as long as we do! I've finished! Let's go to the prayer room before parting, to thank our Creator for his extreme kindness towards us!

Chapter VII

BALANCING THE EARTH
(Constellation of Libra)

"The register of hearts, an exact balance, will appear alongside a rigorous judge.
The tombs will open, and their sad silence, Will soon give way to the cries of the unhappy."

J. DE LA FONTAINE
(Paraphrase of the "Dies Irae").

"Then came an immensity of joy, an ecstasy in which she became absorbed in the rapture she was experiencing: God was there, and she was in him. There was no mystery: all her problems vanished. It's an illumination!

H. BERGSON
(The two sources of morality and religion).

To fully understand the primitive metric system regulating the celestial movements of the Divine-Mathematical Combinations, we must abandon our sordid and debilitating positivism and renew our lost contacts with ancient civilisation! We are currently striving to regulate, according to a purely human concept, what was preconceived and generated according to another Law. For the movements of our sky predate the birth of our race, the so-called human race, to such an extent that it would have taken a super-being living several billion years before the birth of the first humanoid to impose this celestial mechanism, each of whose millions of cogs and gears is a masterpiece of composition! Logically, this presence would also have had to be omnipotent, perpetuating itself uninterruptedly through time to the present day, in order to maintain the precision of the combinatorial movements of the stars.

Arithmetic was twofold, in the sense that to explain Divine Mathematics, one series of sacred numbers was used, and that alone; whereas in everyday calculations, another series was commonly used. A simple example can illustrate this complexity, which is only apparent, for this geometry in space. Among the ancient Egyptians, the calculation system was not decimal as it is today, but duodecimal, i.e. base 12. The numbers 10 and 16 were reserved for Divine Mathematics. They were therefore also reserved for utterances in the Sacred Language, called hieroglyphic in Greek.

The justification for this separation into two distinct categories was explained as follows: "God created the earth on Earth according to his method as Creator, in regular solids of 4, 6, 8, 12, and 20 faces, the only constructions allowed by God to Man his reflection, keeping for himself only basic components such as 7, 9, 10 and 16".

In this way, we have been able to find all the data on the main elevations of the ancient pharaohs. The four-sided tetrahedron, for example, known as the "Pyramid" for some reason, bears in sacred language the much more evocative name of: "Seven-Ben-Mer-Shoum" or "The Beloved-Who-Descends-Light". The double anaglyphic meaning here is obvious, since in the mathematical papyri, Seven means a half-diagonal; Ben, the perpendicular raised into an H; Shou is the edge of the angle providing the cosine. As for Mer, which means "Beloved", it means here an ideal and perfect whole.

The aim of this book is not to study the Numbers, but to explain the astronomical teachings parsimoniously disseminated to the uninitiated by the School of Heaven, known as the "Double House of Life" of Denderah, of which the Golden Circle of the Divine-Mathematical Combinations is the principal element.

Atheist scientists dare not broach a rather thorny contradiction for them, because they would have to allow for too many coincidences, too many disturbing 'coincidences', to justify a random point of view by the grace of Mother Nature alone! This would no longer even be more or less concrete positivism, but an abstract aberration devoid of the slightest foundation. The simple axiom engraved on one of the current walls of the temple of the Lady of the Sky, located at sunset, and tinted pink every evening, is the just counter-indication: "*The Divine-Mathematical-Combinations are the necessities that animate the Law of Creation of the Almighty*".

The Earth's evolution, in perpetual motion, gives birth to and allows the death of all living things within our space, in all times. It eternally renews the foundations that prefigure the life on Earth of men of goodwill whose faith predisposes them to obedience and the Good. The numbers attached to them, and to all things, undoubtedly animate the movements of the Universe according to God's will.

It is certainly easier to smile in mockery at this statement than to take the time to reflect a little more deeply on the real significance of the texts that have been handed down to us at the cost of a thousand difficulties since the dawn of time! But it is true that this state of mind is nothing new, since it is the same in every troubled age. The truth is distorted and hidden under various human masks, where fear finds its nourishment in many forms! The High Priests of the early days of the Golden Circle were well aware of this from their own experience, but it didn't stop them from persevering! They absolutely had to clearly justify the balance of the Earth, which was very precarious because it had already been broken once, upsetting the deepest harmony of the heavens and the stars. What the godless had done, the blind could do again! This abomination would be the final sign of an already decimated humanity.

Did not the Elder of Geb say, during an assembly before the engulfment of Ahâ-Men-Ptah[36]: "The son cherishes his parents less,

---

[36] Extract from Le *Grand Cataclysme*, same author, same publisher.

the wife her husband, the general common love after its own; concord weakens more and more!" And the same facts tended to recur under the same conditions as civilisation advanced within the Second Heart. The balance of the Earth was threatening to break again!

After the assassination of Ahâ Téta, the seizure of power by the usurper, his death at the hands of Téta's eldest son, his marriage to the beautiful and gentle Hen-Nek, Atêta's death following a short, unknown illness ; Hen-Nek, aided by her father Usir-Ka who had become a venerable patriarch, held the sceptre for forty-four years. While Mêna, the first king, reigned for sixty-two years, there were three other Pêr-Ahâ and a queen in the same period. The balance, which was on the verge of breaking, became somewhat tighter during Hen-Nek's reign.

At the same time, the Double House of Life at Denderah was consolidating its teaching, combining the ancient technique of the Elder Heart with the second understanding established in the Second Heart. This essential part was professed by the new Pontiff who had been elected by the College of High Priests, replacing Usir-Ka who was devoting himself solely to running the kingdom as advisor to his daughter, Queen HenKet.

This is why we can practically follow, word by word, all the phrases of this vital part of Knowledge which has to do with the equilibrium of the Earth, and which entered into the meaning of the Combinations within the Twelve, thereafter under the name of: Constellation of Libra.

An-Nu Kâ-Nou-Py, who was the great prophet before becoming Pontiff, knew perfectly well all the intricacies of understanding the sacred texts. And if some of them were open to dispute, that was not the case with this cluster of "Fixes", whose influxes acted as regulators of the earth's equilibrium.

That morning, after the thanksgiving for the rising of the solar globe, the team of teachers gathered in the small private room adjoining the Holy of Holies. It was a good place, and quieter than the others, to assimilate Kâ-Nou-Py's words.

- We are all familiar with the events that preceded the last days of Ahâ-Men-Ptah. They have been amply illustrated in all the texts without the need to return to them. But my prophet predecessors of that distant era were ridiculed and mocked by all when they tried to draw attention to what would happen on a well specified date. The events were so catastrophic that they appeared grotesque and laughable! And yet they took place, despite the violence and abomination they engendered. In truth, few escaped, because few still believed in God and his destructive powers! So what exactly was the situation? That's what we're going to talk about now, if you don't mind.

Spreading a linen cloth across the table in front of him, Kâ-Nou-Py dipped his large reed feathers into the two pots opened for this purpose by his assistants. Then he continued:

- This canvas, which you will have plenty of time to come and contemplate later on, shows all the points of a single observation for a time that may seem exaggerated to you, but is strictly accurate: this cycle is 57,221 solar revolutions, or 39 Sep'Ptah years and 242 solar years. This is obviously not a result of personal calculations. This is a compilation of all the observations made in AhâMen-Ptah, then reported up to now, and verified before being carefully copied down by a Scribe specially trained for this task alone. Several transverse lines provide calculations of the general retreat of space during our popular year, i.e. six hours and five hundred and fifty-one seconds for this period, the cycle of which takes place in 1,423 revolutions, i.e. from the top to the bottom of this canvas. Please take note of these figures, which will be very useful for certain verifications.

A rustle of cloth indicated that all the priests were shaking themselves to pick up their quills and write on the papyrus unrolled in front of them what had been asked of them. After this short pause, the Pontiff resumed:

- A second series of transverse lines, this time red, only two of which are complete, since the general retreat in space calculated for an exact year, according to the conjunctions of Ra-Sep'Ptah, gives a return to the same point in 25,855 solar revolutions[37]. This gives an annual difference of one thousand two hundred and twenty seconds per year. Finally, the third recession occurs in five hundred and fifty-one seconds per year, and it could only have one line since its return only occurs once every 57,221 years, which provides the key to the authentic observations of our astronomical ancestors. The drawing reproduced on this cloth is therefore the linear construction of the Trinitarian pulsations of our celestial Heart, the very pulsations that enable us to solve all the problems that usually arise when we make our combinatorial predictions. A few calculations, restricted to the simplest rules of arithmetic and based on the different lengths of the cycles, lead to a certainty comparable to that with which their duration is determined. In all the cases that will be submitted to you, a copy of this very precious document will have the immense and undeniable advantage of serving as an exploratory field for all the celestial navigations that are still uncertain because of their change of course, and will thus prevent you from deviating from the combinatorial proposals that you have been taught for all the births to be studied. In this way, thanks to the markers at the top and at the side, you will have no difficulty at all, immediately, on each set-back line of the different years, in finding the correspondences with the degrees of the natal chart of the year studied for more than two hundred centuries and for another thirty millennia! From this you will be able to deduce with complete certainty the various locations attributed to a given birth in its relationship with the great circle and the Twelve which encircle it, and this for all known times past or to come!

Satisfied with this tirade, which provoked many murmurs of astonished surprise, the Pontiff continued without further ado:

- The meeting of the lines of recession also determines the length of the most diverse periodic cycles. For example, the

---

[37] In normal round figures, the big year is: $360 \times 72 = 25,920$.

precessional recession meets that of the Sep'Ptah year every 47,172 years. In the same way, it is easy to see, for any given period, the number of days elapsed between the solstice and a given day in any annual cycle. All you have to do is count the number of lines representing degrees on the line of height to obtain the result between the two traces of backward movement. Thus, everything is in the Law of Divine Creation, whose universal mathematics on its cosmic scale required, in order to ensure its faithful reproduction in the first Golden Circle of Ath-Mer, observation at every moment for millennia and millennia before the planned engulfment of our first motherland. The balance of the Earth had been disrupted, and we had to pay! It is this vital knot of a point of no return that we must never, under any circumstances, cross again, on pain of losing our balance. Every Pontiff who has preceded me since there have been Survivors has made this concern the main object of his meditations. In order to eternally remind all the Cadets of the divine will to see his creatures live in harmony with Heaven, the Masters of Measure and Number gave the constellation preceding that of Leo the name of Nut, the good Virgin Queen, protector of the new Heaven, In keeping with their desire to link past and future influences into a single entity, they retained for the constellation before it the symbol of the Old Heaven ( ), on which they balanced the Earth, thus leaving it to God alone to ensure, in his benevolence, equitable justice. And if Nut saved human beings once, thanks to the birth of the Divine Son Usir, there's a very real risk that it won't happen again. The world, precariously balanced and unstable in the old heavens, must face up to its responsibilities before God. He has indeed signed a new covenant, but the past few years have already demonstrated the fragility of such a promise. The rebels have raised their heads to once again put an idol at the head of their ungodly deeds! We have now decided, in order to avoid a similar recurrence, to institute a Supreme Court. It will rule at the time of each solar entry into this constellation, in a single session lasting the time of the complete passage, i.e. thirty days. All grievances will then be submitted to this court, which will consist of eleven judges from the North and eleven from the South, meeting once in An du Nord[38] and the next time in An du Sud[39]. All problems will then be resolved in the strictest justice, and for the greater good of the two clans of our one people finally united under one name, one sceptre, and one theology: that which comes to us from Ptah, the Creator of us all. For while Osiris was born of Nut, the Queen-Virgin whose name is forever blessed, God allowed Set to be born, conceived by Geb. From this antagonism, which ensured the new balance of the Earth, our Masters of Measurement and Number preserved for our holy writings the symbolism of Nut to represent Heaven, and that of Geb to personify Earth. Gathered together in a character of balance and justice, it is they who, beyond the two pans of the scales, will weigh the actions of each of us. Geb represents the earthly body, without its soul, without its identity as a divine creature. Nut, on the other hand, in his representation of the celestial vault, contains all the dimensions of Space and Time, which are the influxes provided by the Twelve to endow us with a Particle of the Divinity. This is why, with the re-establishment of all our institutions, of all our laws, of Sacred Scripture, the Law of the Creation of the Universe decided by the Eternal was born for the second time. And God resurrected a second time here, to ensure the rebirth of his Second Heart: Ath-Kâ-Ptah.

After this series of sentences had come out of his mouth without any apparent effort, the Pontiff Kâ-Nou-Py paused for a few moments to catch his breath and prepare in his mind the turns of phrase he was about to utter. For while the prophecies struck simple but pure souls, the same could not be said of the strong minds watching him, always quick to question and challenge despite their apparent good-natured servility. However, as the attention was as sustained as ever, he preferred not to pursue the distressing question that came to him from the depths of his soul:

---

[38] Heliopolis.

[39] At that time, it was called Denderah. Then, in Dynasty 11, Thebes usurped the name of the first city in the south for its own benefit.

"How many priests were really Servants of God? So he continued in a more incisive tone:

- God has resurrected in this sacred place of the Golden Circle for the second time, and he must not die again, otherwise his great creative work will come to a definitive end! To avoid such a catastrophe, which would prevent our Divine Parcels from being reborn in fleshly envelopes at the prescribed time, we High Priests must all serve our Creator with all our strength, using all the means he places at our disposal. And the first of these is his Law, one and indivisible in its complexity, but comprehensible and usable thanks to the Commandments specified by Usir just after the Great Cataclysm. It is on this initial principle that I will place particular emphasis today, because God's Justice, with its total fairness, will only be perceptible to the gifted souls that you are, if you imbibe one essential fact: the Truth of God. For it is a profound and sad ignorance to doubt the power of the Lord over our own lives! It would be an odious reversal of the rules he instituted and of the Covenant accepted by our repentant Ancestors with regard to harmonisation between Heaven and Earth, and therefore between the Creator and his Creatures. This is the Truth, and it would be iniquitous to attempt to contest the marvellous events that are revived in our Holy Books, by versions that tend to transform them into abominable myths and legends. This is a very dangerous subversive mode for the future of all of us, in which common sense unfortunately loses its rights. Because the history of our Elders is so far removed from our present, it is fading into the mists of time over the centuries and millennia. So we need to put a stop to fairytales, so that they don't become mythology. Truth must be respected, even if it only depends on texts copied after our Elder Heart was swallowed up. In order to avoid one day discovering flaws that do not exist in it, this original Tradition must be preserved intact. The Universe in its present form, as we discover it in its 3,240 celestial aspects, is still the best that exists to ensure us a just and healthy life. And the Law that created it is indispensable to its maintenance, just as Man is necessary to this whole. And while Evil is a human necessity before we can attain the Good, the Great Cataclysm has cleansed us of Evil. It is now up to us to do everything we can to reach the Good. And it's clear that we'll only get there if you all teach the historical truth and not mythological fiction! Faith in our one, eternal, all-powerful God, governor of the universe, is the foundation of our monotheistic theology. Do not look to our texts for the vision of a bizarre chronology where none exists! Don't be tempted by the ridiculous stories of solar paganism. Only our manuscripts are authentic. It's true that you'll find what can only be described as miracles on every page. But miracles are by no means myths! The exemplary account of the lives of Geb and Nut, and the births of Osiris, Set, Isis and NekBeth, are all marvels that can be explained very well if we accept the omnipotence of God. The relationship between the Eternal One and his people in Ahâ-Men Ptah was a rare privilege. It was justified by the Creator's love for his creatures linked to him by the Divine Parcels. Evil, having triumphed in the necessity that it instituted in spite of itself, then allowed the regeneration of humanity with the redemption of the human race with Osiris. All our ancient Masters, the preservers of the Word, those who passed it on to us, did not know our hesitations, our prevarications, our disputes, because they had lived what they were recounting. They were stating real facts without trying to convince anyone of their reality! Trying to find myths in our Sacred Books is as unfounded as trying to prove that Ra is the only food for our intelligence! And if our Elders have lost the Eden that was theirs in Ahâ-Men-Ptah, we must see this only as a momentary triumph of Evil, in order to better fight it later. Unfortunately, it is trying to reappear in its many hypocritical forms, and we must fight it in every way we can. It is indisputable that the existence of moral evil is one of the scourges of the earth! All our Masters have tried to explain this painful phenomenon and to reconcile it with the Good, which is our goal. If everything is God, everything should be good, that's a fact, and that's what I will always preach. But one of man's creations has been solicited by Evil: Set! Jealousy and envy won out over the need for Divine Law. Man was created to live happily, innocently and freely in Ahâ-Men-Ptah. Set seriously abused this freedom by attempting to kill Osiris and his son Horus. As punishment for this sin, he lost everything, but was given a second and final chance to redeem himself. We must never lose sight of the fact that we are created in the image of the Creator, by Himself, just as the jug that holds the water was made by the hands of the potter. Ptah is the divine modeller. By developing, refining, embellishing and modernising our ability to move, to think and to imagine, he has set mankind on the right path. But it can also destroy in an instant, by the mere result of anger, what once thought of itself as sublime majesty! This is how we must aim for the Good, and only the Good, by putting the ancient Commandments back into use. For the substance of the story that has been handed down to us is true, as we can never say often enough. It is still vividly remembered by all of humanity. Our annals record in some detail the memory of our paradise of Ahâ-Men-Ptah. From this golden age, our Elders have left us the memory of a nature of integrity, of the fortunate time when the spirit of God breathed with force over all things and all living beings. So humans had no knowledge of Evil. This is undoubtedly why the divine plan, designed to restore the shattered Harmony, consisted in bringing about a new order in heaven by navigating in the opposite direction to the previous one, thus enabling the Survivors, our Blessed Elders, to rise above the burning ruins to overcome the bottomless abyss of hellish death. The help given by Nut, who became the Lady of Heaven, to perfect and consolidate redemption, no more offends the resurrection of her son Usir than the death of her other son, Set, offends her divinity. On the contrary, by glorifying her wisdom, she aroused Ptah's mercy. The two brothers of the same mother acted only as instruments of the Creator's eternal power on Earth. If this sign was denied despite its obviousness before the Great Cataclysm, it is so clear to us that we would have to be blind not to admit its veracity. Truth and Justice: these two poles of earthly harmony must guide your studies of the Divine-Mathematical Combinations. This is why we will soon use the symbolism of Libra as an image for this constellation. It will be much more striking for the mind. Indeed, when the antagonisms of the two opposing clans, Usir and Set, are weighed up during the month devoted to dispensing justice, they will discover the right balance to their differences at the centre of the scourge! There will no longer be opposition, but union, in the best of all worlds, which will remain ours forever. And let's not forget that our earth is a globe. Not only does the symbolism of the circle balancing on the sky show this, but we have it formally from our Ancestors who describe it to us at length in the Sacred Texts. The Earth is a very large ball suspended in the sky, just like the Sun and the Moon when we see it as a whole. This is why our globe, and not the Sun, will mark the beginning of our combinatorial movements, because the representation of the Earth will be, arithmetically and geometrically, by the sign O. Indeed, when God created the Earth, it was devoid of all elements. It came out of nothing, but there was nothing on it yet. It existed, but *it was empty!* So the empty circle will represent what we all were in the beginning, i.e. nothing. The Sacred Language forms a whole that comes to us from a single source: Ptah the One. Usir passed it on to us through his blessed son Hor. To better meditate on each of these teachings, it is best to think about them very deeply while reading them, because when we talk about them, when I quote one at random in my sentences, each word can be interpreted differently by those who simply listen to the sounds. It is only my mouth that utters the holy words that you hear. It is not my soul that gives you the meaning, but my heart that makes you feel their effectiveness and generosity. Here too there are two conceptions of the Word. If I tell you that I see you in front of me, that's visual reality, because you are there; but if I also tell you that I see what your minds are thinking at the moment, you'll start laughing straight away! Because even if I read some of your ideas in the visible light of your eyes, I idealise or distort the impalpable content of your Divine Parcels as I see fit, depending on my temperament at the time. The word can therefore be twofold, whereas the Law is unique in its sacred transcription. This is the whole that forms Knowledge. That's why only a special elite can have access to it, after passing through many equally delicate initiations! You are privileged in the sense that you are Wise Men in every sense of the word. And unfortunately, that number will hardly increase over the years. Knowledge is like a very strong drink taken too quickly! It intoxicates and clouds the mind. The adept then believes himself to be the equal of a false god, and becomes capable of the worst extremes. Intelligence is made in such a way that few creatures can resist the vertigo produced by this immense Knowledge. This is why our great Sages from the ancient times of the Divine Triad, and then their Successor Servants, deliberately chose this form to transmit the Law to us: in the form of symbols, Numbers and parables, so that ordinary mortals could not have access to it. Even for us who are here in perpetual communion with God and his commandments, how many difficulties do we not encounter in our search for the Truth! But it's not up to us to argue or to rebel: we have to draw additional strength from them in order to succeed in our earthly task. Let's ask our good Lady Nut to help us. She is the patroness of this constellation, Libra.

Quite satisfied with his dissertation for the day, the Pontiff gathered up his brushes to leave the fabric spread out on the table clearly visible to all eyes. His assistants hastened to remove the various feathers. Then he continued:

- It only remains for me to conclude, before allowing you to join me in studying these astronomical calculations, with a simple prayer worthy of the name, dedicated to Nut. We will meditate on it silently. This prayer alone will rise in harmonious union with the Creator's thought. It alone would be capable of pleading the cause of our impious and blind brothers. The prayer of a few righteous people can sometimes bring about a recovery from an imbalance. Let us pray!

Portico at the entrance to the temple at Denderah.

Hypostyle hall of the temple of Isis

Details and study of a pillar with the head of Isis from the Hypostyle Hall.

Chapter VIII

THE SKY GODDESS
(The Constellation of the Virgin)

> *"Earth to heaven, man to Deity, are joined in a new marriage: God, taking body without offending the body, is born today of virginity."*
>
> Joachim Du Bellay
> *(From Christmas Day.)*

> *"On a river called the Bassin de l'Ouest, large boats float. Some sail or row, carrying a large crew. The others have a closed kiosk in the middle."*
>
> Auguste Mariette
> *(The tombs of the Old Kingdom).*

The eleventh Pêr-Ahâ since the time of Mêna, the first, was an "Elder": An-Neter[40]. According to the annals, his reign began 359 years after the re-establishment of the Atêta calendar, which also re-established the Sacred Language. Curiously, An-Neter's father took Neb-Râ as the name of his sceptre-bearer, in order to appease the quarrelsome spirit of the powerful rebels[41], as it meant: "I am the Sun". But it was also he who legalised the worship of the *Hapy* Bull in Men-Nefer, his capital[42]. Usir, the son of Ptah, could not be worshipped in his human image, which could not be drawn or

---

[40] According to Manetho, followed by the chronologists, it was Binôthris.

[41] These were the 'Sun worshippers', descendants of Set.

[42] It was the capital of Ptah, phonetised Memphis by the Greeks, whose lustre was once again dimmed in favour of An, on the other bank of the Nile, which was the Heliopolis of its Hellenic name.

engraved. The symbolism of the bull, thanks to the skin that had saved him from putrefaction, had thus been deified as his reincarnated "Kâ".

The following episode takes place during the sixth year of the reign of the Pêr-Ahâ An-Neter, whose hieroglyphics meant: "I am the descendant of the Eldest, the First-Born". It was his glorification to be, still at that time, the direct Cadet of Mêna. This whole account is historically accurate. The re-established legislation would last until the end of the country, in other words for another four thousand years. His Pontiff was called An-Nou: "the First of Heaven". He re-established astronomy in a less hermetic context, simplifying the iconography used until then.

An-Neter brought immense joy to An-Nout, by decreeing, at the most propitious moment of the Divine-Mathematical Combinations, and with rigorous meticulousness, the institution of matriarchy in the Royal House of Egypt. This was the ultimate glorification of Nut, the Virgin Queen, who gave birth to Usir without the human seed of her husband, but with divine grace, thus implying female supremacy in the transmission of Power and the Royal Sceptre, the two symbols, celestial and terrestrial, of the future Pêr-Ahâ.

And so it was that, from the year BC, all the future "Pharaohs" married the holder of the power of Nut, their "Virgin Mother", even if she was their elder sister, in order to be able to reign themselves. This was in no way to commit incest, but solely to obtain the Power and the Sceptre from the Divine Nut, the Protector of the Elders of Uzir.

That morning, An-Neter, who had every reason to be satisfied with the news he had received the previous day from the distant capital of the North, had just completed the collective prayer in the great Temple of the Sky Goddess, reading the ancient prayers from the carefully preserved Sacred Texts. After returning the "Book", made from ancient papyrus scrolls, to the Sanctuary, and thanking the Creator for his blessings, he had returned to the future Masters of Measurement and Number who had waited to accompany him.

The Pontiff had announced an important decision by the PêrAhâ that would change life in this second homeland, bringing it closer to the ancient traditions of their "Elder Heart": the First.

As soon as they had settled into the room reserved for the Combination lessons, An-Nout began to teach the future teachers this primordial lesson in theology, relayed by Ousir himself. The Pontiff could not help but notice the jubilation in his voice, even though his face remained impassive:

- Yesterday, 365 and a half solar revolutions ago, the Elder Têta re-established the counting of time marking the flight of days and nights, after his father had unified this land promised to our ancestors by Ptah, as a sign of the Covenant. Mêna and Têta will remain until the end of time as the first of our Pêr-Ahâ. But we must never forget, and this is the purpose of our written annals, the History of our "Elder Heart": Ahâ-MenPtah. Nor should we erase from your memories the names of the pioneers who lived for four millennia, between the moment when our Motherland was swallowed up and the arrival of the survivors on the banks of this Celestial River. Let us pay a special and vibrant tribute to Ank-Kâ-Hor, the first Master of Measurement and Number, the Master of you all, who recalculated all the positions of the Wandering and the Fixed in the sky, so that our chronology restarts exactly at the moment that is most harmonious for us. But before this Prophet who lived at the time of Teta, you must remember in particular the venerable Pontiff Bâ-En-Pou, who drew up the definitive plan for the 3,240 chambers of the Twelve of the Celestial Belt, whose construction work began exactly 365 more solar years before Teta. So it's been precisely half a Sep'ti revolution today, or 730 and a half years, that we've been continuing the story of our "Second Heart", following the harmonisation God wanted to bring us back to life according to His rhythm. This cosmic palpitation, the scale of which is beyond us in its infinite grandeur, is nonetheless best suited to making our Parcels of divinity vibrate in unison with the Creator. Those who reject this simple fact are the impious who prefer to worship the Sun, and accept the droughts and famines for which it is responsible because of the blasphemies it causes. By accepting Sep'ti, symbolised by Nut's daughter Iset, we give thanks to Ptah. And on this doubly sumptuous day, it's good to remember the story of our good Queen Virgin, the Good Lady Nut.

Before continuing further, An-Nout smoothed his beard to better classify the order of the heroic events of that distant time when the Queen with the name blessed a thousand times gave birth to the Eldest Son. The passage of time seemed to wear away the reality of the facts, and it was necessary to fight against this progressive erasure in people's minds of a concrete materiality that is historically proven by the annals. With his scheme clearly in mind, the Pontiff continued:

- The important decree issued by the Ahâ An-Neter, which comes into force today, by giving primacy to women in all inheritance rights, has once again legalised the most ancient divinity. In our studies of Mathematical Combinations, we shall also dissociate the double symbolisation of the Virgin Nut. The Fixes of the Belt of the Twelve who bore this Name a thousand times holy before the Great Cataclysm will continue to bear it. But, for the geometrical interpretation of the Mathematical Combinations included in the Golden Circle, we will from now on adopt its figuration in the form of three ears of corn. They will thus symbolise in all minds the Divine Triad, while materialising the primordial fact that was the multitude procreated by Nut in a second stage during her earthly life with Geb. This will be explained in greater detail in your courses, as the Golden Circle is set back in relation to the Belt of the Twelve[43]. Let's return to the chronology of events that you will later have to teach yourselves. You have all learned that a first dynasty of Ahas held the Sceptre in Aha-Men-

---

[43] Today, astrologers (sic) say: "The natal chart moves backwards in relation to the zodiac". Thus, as early as 11th Pharaoh, there was a distinction between the Ears and Virgo, although the basis of calculation was the same.

Ptah for 13,420 years[44]. Ptah had allowed the first Ahâ[45], whose original name was given to him by his Creator himself, Usir, to have an earthly wife. The Almighty had judged that the time had come to elevate certain carnal envelopes to a higher condition. So Uzzir took a wife from among them, in order to procreate a population capable of receiving the celestial spiritual Parcels dispensed by her father. In this way, the first Nut took on her human form when she herself received a soul. After this first period of 13,420 years, the second, which was also well-defined and began after a flood and ended with the Great Cataclysm, lasted 11,520 years. This second dynasty saw the organisation and decline of the people chosen by God to be bearers of Parcels of his creative intelligence. The annals have preserved for us the prestigious names of the dynastic chiefs of that time: Ptah-NouFi, Méri-Ptah-Kaï, Maât-Ptah-Kaï, Ath-Ahâ-Ptah and Hêtet-Ptah-Ti, whose first Ahâ was Geb, who perished gloriously in the Great Cataclysm. This period, although remote, is the one that remains best engraved in our minds, because it has been reproduced on all the walls of our temples. It must remain so eternally if we are to save our souls from the decomposition and putrefaction to which they would be doomed if we no longer believed that God alone is their Creator, Shaper and Owner. Right from Geb's birth, it was prescribed and predetermined that he would be the last Ahâ of this "Heart" so beloved of God, but which he would pulverise! And the Pontiff of that time, as the venerable An-Nu possessor of the Great Secret, never stopped until he knew where the woman destined to become his wife had been born, so that their offspring would find favour with God and not perish when the Motherland was swallowed up. Priests were sent to all corners of the blessed kingdom, and even beyond. This young girl was found on the very day she turned ten. As for Geb, he had just turned twelve. There was no doubt about the young woman's predestination, for her name was Nut, just like that of the first mortal who had married the Elder almost twenty-five millennia

---

[44] All the details are amply revealed in *Le Grand Cataclysme* by the same author, Ed. Omnia Veritas.

[45] Ahâ is spelt Ahan. It is curious that the first man was already called Adam!

earlier. What's more, she was a princess of royal blood, a distant Elder of her father's having reigned over the Province of the Far North, which was submerged during the Flood of early times. Since then, the entire princely family had lived in seclusion, waiting for the Prophecy to be fulfilled, which would make the young child "the Virgin of millions of children". And the miniature drawing that the future king received from the charming young Nut on his eighteenth birthday set his heart on fire. However, with God's wrath approaching and events rushing ahead, it was not until three years later that he took both the Sceptre and the Bride.

As the Pontiff addressed the passage that was least easy to admit, and yet reflected the exact truth, he drew a breath to make the sound of his voice even more incisive. He held out an accusing index finger to the future Masters of Measurement and Number:

- All of you here know by heart this decisive phase in the history of Ahâ-Men-Ptah, which was so fraught with consequences! And I am convinced that there is at least one of you, if not more, who doubts in his heart of hearts, if he does not admit it to himself, the reality of what happened to the princess Nut on the eve of her marriage to Geb. And yet, every word of our Sacred Text concerning this holy episode in the life of the Virgin Nut is the expression of a total truth, from which no fragment can be removed or changed. It is the Truth and nothing else! I must repeat it to you once again, word for word, knowing it by heart in all its miraculous beauty, in its divine form. Bringing his hand to his body, the Pontiff then spoke in a prophetic voice, the better to assert the past reality, the basis of all primordial theology:

- The young Princess Nut, who loved to stroll with her attendants in the cool undergrowth of the Royal Palace, was also there on the eve of her wedding. But that day, she went much deeper into the foliage of the age-old trees. So much so that the future queen came to a wooden bridge that gave access to the Nahi: the Sacred Enclosure that enclosed the Isle of Sycamores, which only the Ahâ could enter, for only he could converse with God, his Divine Father, whom he met in this privileged place. The delightful Nut was, of course, well aware of the rules forbidding entry, but as she reached the little bridge at that precise moment, the nerves of anticipation for the next day, the day of the wedding, combined with tiredness and a little curiosity, made her feel pushed forward as if by an invincible force! And the rest of this extraordinary adventure proves that everything was also written in heaven, so that even if the face of the Earth was turned upside down, human life would continue. And the new humanity was no more discerning than its predecessor! This is why the extraordinary and unbelievable nature of the event is apparent today to those who refuse to recognise God as their Almighty Father! For all of you, as for me, this adventure of Nut's is normal, credible and quite ordinary, since it will be repeated in the future, as our prophecies assure us. God will have to ask another Son to save his Creatures, just as the blessed Nut was about to become Uzir's envelope! For the princess knew nothing of what was to come, and even if she had, she would certainly not have shirked her destiny, as she prepared to set foot on the bridge of bois. An officer from the royal guards, who was protecting the group of young women from afar, quickly approached his future queen to prevent her from committing a terrible sacrilege. Like a good soldier, he respectfully told her that she was forbidden to cross the river, on pain of the worst divine evils. The Nahi, the dregs of the Sycamores, contained only sacred trees, the oldest of which dominated the mound in the centre of an immense foliage, so the good princess would find no place to walk in this holy place. And once again God inspired Nut, accentuating her stubbornness. A magnificent smile appeared on her lips, while a look as warm as it was innocent covered the face of the suddenly embarrassed soldier. The man blushed with shame at his audacity in forbidding this goddess anything! He had no right to interfere with the wishes of the future queen, who from the very next day would be the equal of the king, her Master. She would bear the title of Divine Successor. So there was nothing to stop her from meditating with God. God undoubtedly inspired her, and Nut, as if reading him, added that her followers would await her return in the company of the officer of the guards, the latter remaining mere perishable mortals, which was no longer the case for her. The officer felt an immense sense of heartbreak. That's what the Holy Text tells us about him. But it certainly wasn't the future of the good princess that he was concerned about. Rather, it was his own future compromised by what he imagined to be the escapade of a young girl curious about the forbidden! The command he held would be taken away from him when he reported back. But as he was never mentioned in print again, the ladies in Nut's suite had to calm him down and silence his conscience. Especially as the events that followed had more effect than anything he could have said back at the Royal Palace! For as soon as she crossed the bridge, the princess felt her will dissolve. A strange calm came over her, like a premonitory dream that she had had and that had come true. It was something she had already experienced, probably something terrible and incredible, but something that was bound to happen. She moved forward mechanically. She propelled one leg in front of the other, watching them go like that, as if it wasn't her who was walking there. She was sinking into the Nahi, towards the precise end of her journey, like the end of a long wait. The path climbed, winding around the central hill. It was a large mound, encircled by a winding path that sloped gently upwards. When she reached the top, the enormous sycamore tree, far more enormous than any maple tree she had ever seen, filled her eyes, striking them with a strange glow! The tree was so imposing, in its unquestionable domination of the island's landscape, that the solitude surrounding it emanated an almost palpable divine call to her! And there is no doubt that the serenity of the place allowed all the Ahâ who had come there to talk to their Heavenly Father to speak to him. Nut was invincibly drawn to the tree. Even if she had wanted to, she would not have been able to stop herself from crossing the few metres that still separated her from it. But nothing could hinder the historic course of the earthly journey that the Divinity was about to breathe into her. Good Nut no longer had any doubts about the force that was driving her to come close to this giant sycamore tree. But that did nothing to help her understand the reason for this "Mystery". She was alone, surrounded by total silence. As soon as she was completely under the foliage that darkened everything, an insurmountable fear took hold of her whole body and she began to tremble. It was not the coolness of this phantasmagorical shadow that troubled her, but the incomprehension of what she, a humble mortal, was doing there, insignificant in spite of her role as Geb's wife. For she clearly felt that she was there to bring about something as magnificent as it was irrevocable for the rest of her earthly life. And even though she was distraught at not seeing or hearing anything, she stood up like a proud Nordic princess who no longer admits to *not knowing anything!* And the Sacred Texts tell us that Nut in turn opened up a dialogue: she spoke to God. She told him that she was there, submitting to his will. But the princess received no reply. It was quite clear that this sentence did not require one, since God knew that she was present and under his permanent domination, whether she knew it or not, and whether she wanted to or not. However, the future queen did not understand this silence. She was still too young for the Almighty to reproach her for the slightest sin. It couldn't have been the minor offence of entering the Nahi that had aroused God's anger, especially as she was well aware that she had reached the sycamore against her will. God didn't want her any more, or else she had been foolishly imaginative! She had made up her mind: there was nothing to look forward to, and no one to see! There is certainly much more to be said about this passage of the text, but that is not the purpose of this narrative, which is intended to remind you why Nut was divinised on a day like the present, many millennia after the actual events of the present day.

An-Nu An-Nout had now reached the vital moment of the story. And, as always when he recounted the events, he felt deeply moved, as close to this admirable young woman as he was to God at those moments. He continued:

- The future queen felt weary and a little dizzy from having assumed too much about what would happen next. So she let herself fall onto the thick grass that grew thickly under the trunk of the giant tree. She strained her ear once more, but her particularly receptive soul "heard" nothing! Out of nervous exhaustion, she leaned her hair back against the bark of the splendid trunk, so old and so welcoming to her rest. At the same time, her whole head rested in the shade of the sycamore. From that moment on, the princess's body and soul were at peace. The outside world no longer existed: Nut had closed her eyes without realising it. In this unreal sleep, she dimly realised the event. Her astonishment turned to surprise, then to insurmountable fear, as a radiant, blinding, enveloping light penetrated her interior through every pore of her skin and every opening in her face and body. The most intense fear seized her, although she was unable to move or scream, because she felt as if she were being consumed, reduced to ashes! She told herself she no longer existed, but at the same time she thought she was living the most radiant day the Earth had ever known since its origin. Her intense nervousness was suddenly replaced by a great calm. She tried to open her eyelids, but couldn't even wiggle her eyelashes. She felt herself sinking into a fatalistic unconsciousness, telling herself that what had to be done would be done. A voice confirmed this and tried to comfort her. It was the Voice, the Word and the Word of all time. Nut heard it in the depths of her being, very firm, but infinitely gentle and reassuring, saying to her: "Usir, my Son, now grow in your fleshly body to become 'He who saves from the waters'. Fear not, for you are the one I have chosen to be his Mother. Ousir, through you who will be queen tomorrow, will remain the sign of my Goodness as much as of my Power. You will be revered as one of my daughters for having been Usir's mother. You will teach him, when he is old enough to hear, that he is my son and that part of my immense heart is in him. For this reason, and whatever may happen to him on the part of a human being, he will keep eternity for his Kingdom!"

Pausing for a moment, the Pontiff let these divine words soak into the intelligent brains of the future Masters. For Usir had indeed become the Judge of the dead, the undisputed Master of the Parcels of those who wished to reach the Beyond of Earthly Life. It was a truth as obvious as that concerning the procreation of the Queen-Virgin by God. Then An-Nout continued:

- The admirable princess was incapable of uttering the slightest sound, but she coordinated her thoughts very precisely with a cohesion that disconcerted her on this exceptional occasion. God had announced to her that she would give birth to a child of God: that was good. But the question that came to her mind was so acute that it quickly reached the Lord: "What would become of her if she became Geb's wife the next day? What would Ahâ say when she told her husband the truth? Because she couldn't hide it from him even if God wanted her to...". And the Eternal One, in response to this silent and desperate appeal, decided to come to her aid immediately. A broad ray of sunlight filtered down from the top of the gigantic sycamore to the lowest branches. The sudden warmth invigorated Nut. She once again heard the Voice conversing with her within this aura that was as luminescent as it was silent. For so long, God was speaking to her:

"Fear not, Nut, rise up and go in peace to the one who has always been destined for you, so that humanity may survive. Geb is now receiving my Word and he will obey my command. To do this, after Usir, the descendants of both of you will include a Son of the Earth: Usit. And from these two offspring will arise all the possibilities of Good and Evil, which will be the essence of the free choice of the new path that humanity will undertake in its pursuit of eternal life. But while you wait for this second departure, go back to Geb, who is already running to the Nahi, for I have already told him everything! With these last words, the spell that seemed to paralyse Nut faded. The princess opened her eyes without surprise. Nothing around her seemed to have moved; even the half-light had reclaimed the spot where she was still sitting. A little dizzy when she stood up, she only regained her balance as she approached the little bridge. For her future husband was arriving, dishevelled and panting from his hasty run from the castle after God had spoken to him.

And this was happening just as Nut's attendants, worried about their mistress's prolonged absence, were asking the officer of the guards to send for the king. The sight of the monarch calmed them all, especially as he, having a general view of everyone, resumed a gait more worthy of his rank, although he retained a rigidity in his movements that appeared to everyone to be a bad omen! When the good Nut saw this, she was even more disturbed and slowed down, hesitating about what she should do and say. I won't dwell on the rest of this event, for it was undeniably reminiscent of the story of the first Ahâ and his wife Nut, whose child was an Uzir several millennia earlier. Geb and the second Nut were the innocent and involuntary victims of the madness that had devastated all the Souls of the Elder Heart of God. They married not only to obey the divine commandments, but because they loved each other deeply, beyond all human vicissitudes. And so Usir was born in his own time, at the appointed hour. Then it was Usit's turn. Both brothers were born of the same mother, Nut, but while the elder was of divine essence, the younger was born of earthly seed. All the Good of the first and all the Evil of the second would make our humanity and this second homeland where we are what it has unfortunately become! But Nut will remain eternally the Mother, the Goddess, the Virgin Queen from whom the multitude was born. And the resemblance with the first Nut was such that the Masters of Measurement and Number, the survivors of Ahâ-Men-Ptah, did not deem it necessary to create a new iconography to immortalise the divinity of this second Nut, who replaced the first in the cycle of the Twelve of the Celestial Belt without any difficulty, or damage, in the backward countdown to the new times after the Great Cataclysm.

The Pontiff mechanically rubbed his hands in satisfaction at having successfully told this true story, which was already tending to turn into something of a fanciful legend. The most difficult thing would certainly be to keep the Texts in the Future strictly real. His successors would have a hard time of it! Perhaps they themselves would begin to have doubts... An-Nout shook himself so as not to foresee prophetically what might happen. He continued in a less impassioned tone:

- As the sky changed direction without disturbing the order of the Wandering and the Fixed, no particular problems arose. However, the same was not true for the mathematical order of the Combinations in the Golden Circle for the study of each person's destiny. As you have already learned, it is our round Earth that sails through the Heavens around the Fixed Sun. This is easy to understand, even for minds less open to these things of Heaven. The Wandering and the Fixed appear to us rising in the east and setting beyond our sunken Motherland in the west. This is every day that God presents to us in his infinite goodness. It is therefore obligatory, all being order and harmony in the universe, that the Wandering and the Fixed pass under the Earth in another semi-circle in order to make their daily rounds.

Our globe is isolated on all sides, at the centre of the Twelve that encircle it. Our Elders had observed all this and had calculated from father to son the length of a complete revolution around the Belt. This was absolutely necessary for those who knew that God legislated according to a single law, on His own scale. By dint of patience and tenacity, in order to live in harmony with Heaven, our ancestors on Earth managed to determine the length of this year. Here too, although unverifiable during a human lifetime, the figure of 25,920 years is rigorously accurate. And since we needed a point of reference for this calculation that was more relevant to our lives, the year of God was taken as the fixed point, with Sep'ti as its centre. In this way, the work required by our Covenant with God was made possible in a more precise timeframe, that is, 1,461 years. For Ra's navigation gives no accuracy in the calculations, still less a comparative scale with the work of Divine Creation. From this 25,920-year backward movement of the Sun in relation to the Earth, the different irradiation of the Twelve of the Belt on the Earth's atmosphere first, and then on the human mind, made it possible to construct an outline of the 3,240 original possibilities given by the Creator to his Creatures so that Goodness alone would reign over his Creation. This complex was built at Ath-Mer before the first 'Heart' was swallowed up. It was a repeat of the same complex here, at Ta Nout-Râ-Ptah, but with a different formulation, the retreat instead of the apparent advance of the Sun in the zodiacal constellations having changed the whole predetermination of the human species by the grace of God. As the discrepancy between the Twelve of the Belt and the Twelve of the Golden Circle increases from year to year, and so that there is no ambiguity among the continuators of your teaching who will be your great-grandchildren, each location of the Golden Circle will receive a new symbol. What could be more natural than for the constellation of the Virgin Nut to be symbolised by three ears of corn? Between her two sons, she will symbolise the whole of humanity. Similarly, Nut's virgin body, in a stylised, inverted form, symbolises the sky, as well as her role as Protector of the multitude. This is why she is our patroness and benefactress. She is still demonstrating her power today by having her matriarchal supremacy re-established. I know all this seems pointless to you.

But never forget that our people are already 31,322 years old[46], and that the future will reach the same figure if our people remain faithful to God. I have been the 226th Pontiff since the first An-Nu to survive the terrible cataclysm set foot on Ta Mana. How many more there will be after me, I cannot say with certainty, too many foreseeable hazards and horrors are already coming to light in our Divine-Mathematical Combinations. May they be erased by the understanding and obedience of each human being to the commandments required by the Law of Creation.

---

[46] It is the Eleventh Pontiff who is speaking, hence the difference of 999 years with the chronology of the *Great Cataclysm*.

Chapter IX

THE GREAT CATACLYSM
(THE CONSTELLATION OF LEO)

*"On that day,
The fountains of the Great Deep burst forth,
And the floodgates of heaven were opened."*

OLD TESTAMENT
(Genesis, VII - 11.)

"Thuthmosis III, Pharaoh of the 18th Dynasty, i.e. 2,000 years before Christ, ordered the complete rebuilding of the Temple of Denderah according to the plans of King Khufu (the Khufu of the 4th Dynasty, 1,500 years older still) copied from others much more ancient.

THE ANTIQUITY OF
*(Zeitschrift für aegypterische Sprache,
May 1865, page 92)*

Suddenly, the Sun appeared on the eastern horizon just where hundreds of pairs of eyes were waiting for it. It seemed to sway its molten gold before the blinking eyelids and, very quickly, it tinted the entire site of Denderah with the most vivid colours. The cloak of night had evaporated, giving way to a beautiful day that was shaping up to be very auspicious.

For the ruins of this place would be reborn from the sacrilege that had been committed! An accursed king - not a PêrAhâ - of outrageous mysticism had, in the name of his solar idolatry, ordered the demolition of the temples of Ptah throughout the country, in the north at Men-Nefer, as here at Dendera! Twenty-three years of lowly dictatorship had passed, accentuating the misery of God's chosen people and adding to an already naturally stifling atmosphere. King Khufu[47], if he wasn't growing wiser by the day, seemed to be seeking Ptah's benevolence as much as Ra's since he had been wounded in an ambush during his last war beyond the sea. Seeking to attract all the heavenly graces for his arrival in the Beyond of life, he had given the order to re-establish freedom of worship throughout the kingdom, and even in the two lands: Ath-Kâ-Ptah, and Ahâ-MenPtah.

The Pontiff Khânepou smiled bitterly at this thought, since Amenta was the land of the Sleeping Blesseds, who no doubt could not care less about the earthly decrees of this Sun-worshipper! But the order had arrived the day before, from His Majesty himself, to undertake the reconstruction of the Temple of Nut, the Mother Goddess of the Two Brothers, according to the original plans drawn up by the Followers of Horus long ago. It was his own son, Jedef-Ra, who had brought the papyrus of the royal decree. He was a co-regent, and as such, on this exceptional dawn, he was present at the prayer for the purification of the temple area, where the holy edifice would once again stand, identical to its predecessor.

Having come out of a prolonged retreat, the Pontiff had welcomed this usurping crown prince and his numerous retinue, as was his duty on this occasion. The silent meditation that kept them all in inner dialogue with their 'Kâ' resembled an outward glorification of the sun, but most of them, like An-Nu, had to thank Ptah for granting them this spiritual revenge, to allow this sacred place to rise from the ashes.

---

[47] Khufu was the hieroglyphic name that the Greeks phonetised as Cheops. His story will be told elsewhere, as he was the first great 'rebel' king to regain power by legally re-establishing the cult of the Sun. As he reigned for twenty-three years, this episode takes place shortly before his death.

With the rising of the blindingly bright star, the ceremony came to an end. The Pontiff, quite content to have concealed his repulsion for his illustrious guests, bowed stiffly to the usurper's son, but with the words of farewell required by protocol.

- Long live Djedef-Ra, heir to the god of the Earth and to Nut, the Blessed Goddess of these sacred places. May His Majesty Khufu, born of the sky and of the sun itself, eternally alive, be thanked for the immense benefits he is willing to bestow once again upon this temple dedicated to Nut, Ptah and Ra. May he be granted to live like the Sun, above all and without enemy.

The Pontiff then turned his back on the officials to go to the small temple of Horus, the only monument still standing after the blasphemous madness of this worshipper of the Sun, who had had the walls of all the religious buildings dedicated to Ptah the One demolished. He quickly crossed the pathway between the huge mounds of ruins and disarticulated pillars, followed by his followers who, like him, had had to wait in the shadows of the underground tunnels inaccessible to the false gods for a return that would not come for another twenty years.

On reaching the heavy gateway, sealed with a clay seal bearing the arms of Khoufou, Khânepou smiled as he ordered a young priest in his retinue to break the seal.

Dozens of bats whirled around, chirping at this untimely intrusion, which was unexpected for them to say the least. It smelt musty and rotten, with only a few meagre openings letting in a diffuse light. Everything would have to be cleaned up and the building desecrated by the Sun worshippers would have to be rededicated before it closed.

With sadness rather than disgust, the Pontiff signalled not to go any further and to leave, adding:

- Let's get together to pray and talk for a while in the shadow of the walls of the Holy of Holies. I saw in passing that even this thrice-blessed place is now a ruin!

The sacred boat must be completely crushed under the collapsed ceiling. We'll have a huge job on our hands to ensure that the reconstruction goes ahead as quickly as possible.

With a heavy, heart-rending sigh, the Pontiff turned back. Prince Djedef-Râ and his retinue had already left the square. In a hurry to get back to the festivities in Mennefer, the capital, they had certainly got on board and hoisted the sails! This reinvigorated Khânepou, who moved forward more swiftly, taking care not to stumble over the stones littering his path. When he came to a huge, misshapen heap, he had a hard time convincing himself that, before the destructive madness of the usurper, this was the sacred place where he liked to meditate and recall the glorious past of what had been the Motherland of his ancestors, the Blessed Sleeping Ones.

As the Sun left a spot in the shadow of a large section of wall still standing, the An-Nu made a broad gesture with one hand:

- There's enough room here for our first open-air meeting for twenty years! We need to make up for lost time. It's a good thing this Khufu couldn't find the entrance to the underground passageways leading to the Golden Circle, despite the temple's complete demolition and all the abuses committed against the priests he was able to capture and torture. No one has spoken and our immense treasure is intact in the room dedicated to it. Similarly, all the archives of our four times are still preserved in their entirety. It will be easy for us to rebuild the temple exactly as it was designed by the Followers of Horus, since we still have the plans they drew up for this purpose a little over a thousand years ago. What a mess! The Great Cataclysm that wiped out our Elder Heart six millennia ago must have had a prelude similar to this after the first earthquakes that shook it!

A pout of incomprehension crossed the Pontiff's face before he exclaimed:

- What fault have we committed that God would allow such sacrilege? In what way are we responsible for the impious sun worshippers taking the Sceptre? Must we be punished because of them?

Khânepou shook his head in denial, thus answering his threefold question en bloc. He continued:

- No! Three times no! God wants to ensure our faith, and we're going to show him that he can trust us. For our ruins are far from those left by the Great Cataclysm. By way of meditation, let's take a look at this distant theme, which perhaps we haven't talked about enough during our wait, which has been made up entirely of hope: The An-Nu resumed more briskly after a brief pause:

- You'll all remember the phrase engraved in the Crypt of the Sunset, which I sometimes quoted to you: "The sky is already blushing with the excesses of morals! This is the prelude to the blaze of heavenly fire. Nothing is healthy any more; nothing is wise in Ahâ-Men-Ptah! All her States are infected with impiety and blasphemy! Alas, the time of the Great Cataclysm is at hand! What a terrible time! Your roar from the Lion will break even the Lion's power!

Like him, they all remembered this prophetic passage very well. The Pontiff felt that the time had come to take up this passage from the ancient texts in order to change the name of the constellation bearing the name "Knife", symbolising in everyone's minds the weapon hated by Set the Assassin. It was time to give it back its original name of Leo. He continued in this vein without further ado:

- In rebuilding the Temple, we will modify the characters designating the constellation of the Great Cataclysm. We will give it back its original all-powerful symbolism. Moreover, the Knife must be erased from everyone's minds as quickly as possible, since the child of Set who now holds the Sceptre has made amends for his sins against the only God who holds celestial power. The warning given by the Lion will be reinstated in the languages of our Elders. A retrospective of the catastrophic events of this shocking period in our history will do us a great deal of good by reminding us how little we are in God's hands. So it was during solar navigation in the constellation Leo, during the normal advance of the Great Year. Time was running out, and in his omnipotence, the Creator was going to punish his creatures for the unspeakable sins they had committed. The first tremors of the ground had already occurred, and mankind was trembling with anguish and fear, but too late in its spiritual remorse! The rescue of the people, though meticulously planned and prepared by Geb, was becoming too uncertain to be carried out. The people tried, but a little too late, to leave their homes, their lands and their most cherished possessions, to embark with no resources and with their families, towards an unknown destination. The rigorous order that should have governed the attempts to embark on the Mandjits, those famous unsinkable boats that had become the symbol of the rebirth of all and the resurrection of Usir, had given way to the most appalling panic! The terror-stricken crowd had reverted to the savage state they were in before the Divine Parcels were implanted in them! Hand-to-hand combat and jostling brought the advantage back to those who were the strongest. But none of them was yet aware of the sheer scale of the rift that was about to occur! Two hundred kilometres from the blessed capital, Ath-Mer, the volcanoes were suddenly gripped by hellish contractions. Underground fires that had been smouldering for millennia came to light. And the internal pressure was such that they spread a monstrous torrent of powdery lava and ash all the way to the clouds, where it coalesced into an opaque fog and fell as far as the capital, inexorably and implacably covering it with an indestructible mantle. A solid rain piled up, engulfing those who had the misfortune to stop for even a second in their desperate flight. Chunks of rock and rubbish of all kinds fell on the crowd running towards the port to board the ship, crushing some and knocking others out until they suffocated under the rubble! Hell was breaking loose everywhere...

The Pontiff paused to look at those who, like him, had vowed to be Servants of God, come what may. What would they have done in such circumstances? What would he himself have done? When disaster struck his temple, he hid himself away, waiting for God to come to his rescue, and he was granted his wish. But at the time of the Great Cataclysm, what would he have done and would he have been heard? It was far from certain! He continued:

- The terrible catastrophe foretold by all the Prophets of earlier times was happening. The terror that had gripped them all, and the horror of the event that they had considered incredible and had laughed at so much, was now playing on their minds! They no longer reasoned, and instead of only ten people boarding the boats that were waiting for them, they piled on thirty or more, fighting to get on again, so much so that the unsinkables sank from the excess weight that they contained! So much so that the entire first flotilla of several hundred Mandjits sank, swallowing up thousands of carnal envelopes already stripped of their Divine Parcels. As for those who had huddled in their homes in terror, the volcanoes suddenly erupted with thousands and thousands of tons of incandescent ash, which crushed and consumed everything before burying it all! At the same time, Iset and her twin sister were searching for the body of her husband Usir, who had been murdered by Set and sewn into a bull's skin so that his soul would perish and rot with his body, before being thrown into the sea to be eaten by crocodiles. At the same time, Horus had located his uncle Set, the knife-wielding killer, and was preparing to do battle with him. At the same time, the celestial lion was already roaring at the fate that was to be his and that had been planned by God to punish the ungodly. But the final human clash had not yet taken place between those who advocated Evil and those who desired Good. So time seemed to suspend its advance, even momentarily calming the raging elements. Even this delay was not used to try and find a solution that would satisfy the Creator of all things. Set, who for a time had been the man named Usit, took advantage of the lull to try and kill his nephew Horus too. He almost succeeded, breaking his knee bone, dislocating his shoulder and gouging out one of his eyes! Iset, on the other hand, found the body of her husband, which she took back to a Mandjit to board with him. And the cracking of the earth's crust resumed its terrifying concert. In the sky, which seemed to be collapsing in its turn, deafening explosions resounded, their dazzling clarity demonstrating to the living, if proof were still needed, that lightning also belonged to God and to him alone, just like Eternity. As for the last king, Geb, he had ordered Nut, his beloved wife, to leave with her followers without further delay, because another land would welcome the Survivors, who would be in great need of another Mother rather than a King. The violence of the elements unleashed at this crucial moment overcame Nut's hesitations. She nodded at her husband's request, unable to express her despair. She embarked just as a terrible explosion opened up an enormous crater beneath the feet of the many fugitives still trying to reach a starting point to leave this cursed land. The huge gaping hole swallowed up the rest of the living, before vomiting them out a few moments later in the form of ash and lava! Those days were over: the Sun was already suspending its direct navigation in front of the celestial Lion.

The Pontiff closed his eyelids for a brief moment. The almighty power of Ptah, the only one capable of stopping the cogs of celestial mechanics, had shown itself that day to the eyes of the incredulous survivors. And it was not a divine sign, but an earthly reality. There would be nothing left of the Earth that had been Eden for a chosen people, and even the survivors were in danger of being consumed by the horrible heat radiating from the multiple furnaces. Ousir's good mother almost didn't make it either!

With a sad sigh, the An-Nu continued:

- The prayer of our Protector, undisputed Mistress of these eternal places, at the critical moment when the cataclysm was unleashed, was engraved here. We had it in front of us every day, without paying any more attention to it, even though it was also present in our minds. Let us all repeat it in chorus, so that it may serve as an intermediary in our intercession with God, so that he may give us the courage we need to put everything back in order here on earth, according to the Law of the Creator, which has been flouted for twenty long years.

"O time that suspended its flight in a Lion!"

Twenty-three voices became one, repeating with great fervour the phrases of the prayer that Nut had addressed to the One who had begotten her to become the Divine Mother:

- O Ptah-Hotep[48]! You who are the King of Heaven, open the floodgates of your kingdom so that the fire you sent down on Your own beloved Heart may be extinguished! Save your Son's son; save your offspring from hell! Command that this day of the Great Cataclysm does not become the day of the Great Mourning. O Ptah-Hotep! You who are also the King of the Earth, in order to save Horus, the son of Usir, order the Great Celestial River to rain down all its reserves so that those you have spared may be saved!

"Saved, saved, saved"

---

[48] Literally: "God of Peace".

The echo echoed the last word: "saved", "saved", "saved", in many places around, as if to give greater force to the sign of benevolence he bestowed on Nut. In the silence of the once again battered stones, the Pontiff continued:

- And the annals of our Book of the Four Eras contain precisely what happened then. "The Earth darkened again over Ath-Mer, for the prayer of the Virgin Queen had been heard by the Eternal Father. A dense rain began to fall on the molten ground, where it first turned to vapour. Then it quickly accelerated until it became torrential, proving that the very springs of the Great Abyss were emptying! Rain by day, rain by night, and the crackling flames gave way to an ocean of mud! And the last tide swallowed up all those who were unable to leave the shores at that time. It was too late to save the others, who, haggard, their eyes full of the despair of those who had forgotten that they had once been human, had sought a precarious refuge elsewhere than on the Mandjits, the unsinkable lifeboats of divine origin, designed by the Ahâ. For this reason, each temple had a reproduction in its sanctuary, along with a piece of one of the three sacred boats that had saved Nut, Usir and his wife, and Horus. For they had survived by the grace of God. The Son, holding the new Soul of the world in his hands, had floated to the new shore, under a sun still unstably balanced, stopped as it was in mid-heaven. It was not until the early hours of the morning that the ship docked on another unrecognisable land. But the most frightening thing was that the sky *was no longer the same!*

The Son, holding the new Soul of the world in his hands had floated to the new shore.

It was very difficult for humans living six millennia after such a celestial phenomenon to understand what had happened! The Pontiff shook his head, for although he was firmly convinced of the reality of what had happened, he told himself with fear that divine power was immeasurable. For at dawn, the Survivors could no longer recognise 'their' sky: the Sun, which usually rose in the west, had that morning appeared in the east. It wasn't until evening that it set just above a sea that hadn't existed the day before, but which covered this once blessed place in a liquid shroud. God was thus demonstrating that the sun's 'sunset' had become the earthly sunset of a fallen continent. For the Annals, AhâMen-Ptah was now the Amenta: the domain of the Sleeping Blessed, redeemed at the last moment by the Resurrection of Uzir.

The Pontiff shook himself, for it was a glorious day to allow the temple of Nut to rise from its ruins. So he continued in a less mournful tone:

- No! The sky was no longer the same, because the Sun seemed to have changed course from front to back. Although it was still in the constellation Leo, it was no longer moving forwards, but backwards. As a result, east became west. So when the survivors landed in an unrecognisable land, they called it *Ta Mana*[49], because it was from here that they first saw the Sun set over their sunken country. Since God had resolutely manifested himself through the Lion, and in such a bloody manner, it is only natural that this warning should serve to maintain the fear of a similar renewal in all hearts. But it is also normal that the exemplary punishment under this Lion should serve the Ahâ, true Sons of the Creator through their direct descent from Uzir. To distinguish us from the usurpers, I have decided to institute a special Combination which will bring forth all the PêrAhâ during the passage of the Sun in the 31 days of the month of Têta. Our medicine, thanks to the Ahâ Têta, is advanced enough to allow this if a divine baby is early or late in this period. What's more, to ensure that this birth in Leo remains

---

[49] Literally: "Place of the Sunset". This is still the Arabic name for Morocco: Mohgreb-al-Aqsa.

harmoniously in tune with Heaven throughout the King's earthly life, he must be girded with a lion's skin, the tail of which skims the earth, thus linking him to the influences of the Twelve.

And the Pontiff thought that the tail alone, linked by a strap to the waist, would be enough to symbolise this force linking Ahâ to his divine father. But the An-Nu did not specify this last thought, as future kings were likely to quickly make this decision themselves. So he continued:

- The old and the new Leo being intimately linked in the Combinations of our Golden Circle by the reborn life of a second multitude, the sky took its new equilibrium after the Great Cataclysm, and Leo, as Master of the Sky, led the navigation of the Twelve. This symbol will also have another enormous advantage, to which I draw your special attention. I've had enough time to think about it during my long underground retreat. This month of Teta, which is the attractive pole of the L:ion, is also the month when the Sun, at its zenith, has the most calorific influence on the spirits. It dominates all things.

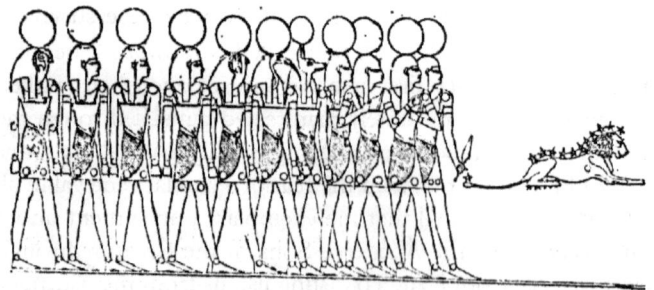

Since the Great Cataclysm, Leo has been leading the new navigation of the Twelve.

If Ra is only one of Ptah's executing arms, some people - and unfortunately we are well placed to suffer the consequences - consider him to be an idol! Leo will therefore be the Master of the Sun on all occasions! It will be the Light of the spirit that shines on the Ahâ. The Lion of the Golden Circle will be so closely associated with the astral Sun that they will become inseparable. And the Sun, which disappears every evening and reappears every morning, gives predominance to the one who is attached to both heaven and earth. It is our utmost concern to ensure that another idolatrous usurper does not return after the one we have. That would be another general ruin from which no one could recover. Another way of avoiding this catastrophe is to safeguard the Golden Circle, by not introducing any black sheep among our Masters of Measure and Number, and this point is relatively easy to satisfy given our initiatory stages. However, we must remain vigilant. The Year of God, identified with the movement of the Sep'ti Fix, ensures our advantage. The idolaters tried everything to use the Combinations derived from its creative geometry in space. But they have never succeeded, because 1,461 solar revolutions varying from year to year present too many difficulties for them, who have no Golden Circle at their disposal. Destructive fury is no substitute for Knowledge.[50]

A smile lit up the Pontiff's face, and he continued in a more mischievous tone:

- Let's go over the astronomy of Sep'ti again, from memory. I don't think I've lost my mind on this subject, despite two decades spent in prayer and meditation in anticipation of what has happened today. The Year of God, which corresponds to the duration of Sep'ti's navigation, to which was given the divine name first of Nut and then of Isis since her arrival on this blessed earth, is very particular in its celestial MathematicalCombinations. This year ceases its revolution when Sep'ti, in its morning appearance just inside the notch on our observatory terrace, is obscured by the rising sun, which itself appears on the eastern horizon, making Sep'ti disappear from our view. As our ancestral Masters were able to observe before us, who merely verified their assertions, it is not necessary for this conjunction to be mathematically achieved for

---

[50] Remember that this is our star Sirius, phonetised in Greek as Sothis. Its primitive hieroglyphic form is (𓀀), which later became (𓀀), or Sept'Iset (Sirius-Isis) and was finally deified (𓀀), i.e. the Divine Sirius-Isis, as found in a text from Denderah (𓀀), which gives a very precise geometric direction in a chamber of the Golden Circle.

the two Fixes to be together on the same point on the horizon. Because of Ra's luminous power, this conjunction takes place when he is eleven degrees below the predicted line at the moment when Sep'ti appears in the notch. It is the annual movement of this crucial point, which moves with each new solar revolution, that determines the start of the year in our popular 365-day calendar. It is also what we use to count the "days" of the Year of God. It also enables us to calculate the "years" of the Great Year. Our venerable ancestors thus observed that each solar year at this point occurred six hours later than at Sep'ti, and that if all the calculations of the Year of God were to be true, it was necessary to add one more day to the solar year every four annual revolutions of Ra, otherwise we would only obtain 1,460 years for the navigation of Sep'ti, which actually comprised 1,461[51]. There is no need for me to add that all these astronomical observations are not speculative, since every day we are able to make these annotations on the live sky ourselves, while waiting for our observatory terrace to be rebuilt. It is obviously thanks to all these operations carried out here, with constant accuracy, that each of my predecessors has written the great History and Chronology of our Elders. It is all these calculations that the solar idolaters envy us and that they will never take from us... if Ptah, in his infinite goodness, remains present in us and with us, despite our lack of faith in him on certain occasions! Our descendants thousands of years from now may no longer understand our hesitations, our spiritual rigour, and even less so the brutal and fratricidal antagonism that separated, and continues to divide, one and the same family into two clans. But God is God, and we are his Prophets, whereas the Sun is and will eternally remain a ball of fire that foolish idolatry is trying to substitute for its One Creator. May Khoufou very soon come to the end of his

---

[51] The point used to calculate the length of the Sirius Year in 1,461 years, and not 1,460, is called the HELIAC POINT in our astronomical language, but it was indeed explained in his own way by the Pontiff. The ancient Egyptians had undoubtedly discovered by their observations alone that the length of the heliacal year was 365 days 1/4. I can imagine that the astronomers of our time, accustomed to modern instruments and methods, have paid little heed to ancient observations. However, if they come down from their heights and go back to the ancient way of observing, the result will be the same. A.S.

time on this earth, and taste in the Hereafter what Ptah will surely have in store for him. That's all for this first reappearance in the shadow of good Ra[52]!

---

[52] Khufu, thus Khufu, lived for another forty years, holding power with a gentle hand.

Chapter X

CADET TIME
(The Constellation of Cancer)

> *"The inhabitants of this country say they have inherited from their ancestors that the sun now sets where it used to rise.*
> C. J. SOLIN
> *(Polyhistor, Chap. 33.)*

> *"We now know that Méri-Râ Pépi had worked at the temple of Hathor, which had existed at Dendérah since the earliest times.*
> EMMANUEL DE ROUGE
> *(Monuments of the first six dynasties).*

What is certain is that an apparent continuity in the confrontations between the two clans, once again fratricidal, became more and more acute as the centuries passed. Khoufou's monuments will be remembered for the hammered names of their builders, whose identity was usurped by his own! This was blatantly obvious at Thinis, where two cartouches bearing his 'label' were nevertheless deciphered under that of the predator. The same thing happened at the famous Great Pyramid of Cheops. Laboratory experiments using Carbon-14 on papyrus cords as big as the wrist, discovered in a cache used as a storeroom inside the pyramid, especially for broken tools, prove that the work predates the despot's reign by more than a thousand years. These tests carried out in Cairo were confirmed by the famous *Chicago Institute,* which had more sophisticated methods at its disposal in the USA. Its results were the same one hundred and twenty years earlier!

The son of this Khufu, Djedef-Ra, reigned for only a few years, followed by his brother, whose pyramid remains. Then came a nobleman who took advantage of the vacancy in power to take the Sceptre: Sheru, who was quickly replaced by his son. This was the

Mykherinos of the Greeks, to whom we owe the third pyramid. Then came his son, who reigned for only four years and had serious cash-flow problems.

From then on, as the priests of Ptah no longer provided their "obols" to a wide variety of kings, the fifth Manethonic dynasty was described as that of Elephantine, an opulent town located between Aswan and the First Cataract, more than a thousand kilometres from Cairo. It seems that some emigrants from this town had come to settle in the capital a century earlier in order to prosper there. They were so successful that one of their grandsons, having risen to the highest rank in the priesthood of the followers of the Sun in An (Heliopolis), married the eldest daughter of the last Ahâ of the decadent Fourth Dynasty. He thus took the Sceptre under the name of Usir Kâ-Rê. Thus began the Elephantine dynasty, this "double Osiris of the Living Sun". This was the true union of the solar clergy with the court of Men-Nefer. Eight kings succeeded him in the same lineage. The last of these was Usir-An, commonly known by hieroglyphic inversion as Ounas. His pyramid at Saqqarah was almost completely ruined when the stones used to build it were appropriated for the construction of beautiful houses in Cairo!

The man who began the Sixth Dynasty is well known physically, as a funerary cast of his face was found in his pyramid in the necropolis of Men-Nefer. His name was Teta, like the Elder who had re-established hieroglyphics. Moreover, the walls of his chamber of accession to the Beyond of earthly life bore the carefully copied primordial data of what became known as "Memphite theology", as opposed to "Tentyrite". But in reality there is no fundamental opposition between the two in relation to solar idolatry, which is considered sacrilegious.

After a short reign of six years, he ceded the Sceptre to a second Usir Kâ-Rê, but who was a solar usurper. He re-established unity in the wrong direction, which led to his own elimination after an eight-year usurpation by a legitimate Aha: Pepi Ier.

It is from this Elder that the history of Denderah is historically perpetuated, despite the apparent contradiction of his divine name, which was:-Meri-Ra, or "the Beloved of the Sun"-.

One thousand three hundred and thirty years had passed since the enthronement of the first Ahâ: Mêna. The third reconstruction of the Temple of Nut had been completed two centuries earlier, but her religious name had become Hathor. This is one of a thousand patronymics attributed to Isis down the ages, just as our Virgin Mary is called not only Mary, but Our Lady of the Springs, of the Storms, of the Snow, etc., depending on where the religious building is erected.

Since Hathor means "Heart of Horus", it was the familiar patronymic of "Good Mother", the heart of Horus obviously being that of his mother. She was by no means another usurping "goddess", as Egyptologists have always written, attributing to her the role of the Greek Venus of love. On the contrary, Hathor was the symbol of maternal love: that of the time of the Cadets.

Nothing was changed in the layout of this third temple, apart from the features of the good Virgin Queen Nut at the top of all the temple pillars, which took on a more human, more peaceful face. The serenity of Hathor's smile was one of her main characteristics, and one that attracted barren women in any case. It is certain that the maternity of Iset, or Isis, "Heart of Horus", of which excellent engravings have been found not only in the last Ptolemaic temple, but also in that of Pepi, was well suited to attracting divine benevolence to this thrice-holy place.

To fully understand how this "Lover of the Sun" became a "Follower of Horus", we need to take a look at the history of this period. Pepi acceded to the Sceptre in 3,014 BC. The people of Elephantine had not only established themselves in the north, but also in the various provinces, or Nomes. Powerful families had risen to regional power, assuming ever greater local importance, and thus limiting their obedience to royal power to attending the sovereign's traditional festivals in his capital, bringing him the magnificent gifts that made them so rich.

And Pepi travelled widely, not only to perfect his knowledge, but also to establish religious buildings where there were none, or to be appointed Royal Priest of existing sanctuaries. His name is written not only at Denderah, but even on a temple in Lower Nubia.

But let's go back to the temple of Hathor, on the last day of Pepi 1er's visit to the site of Dendera. The officiating Pontiff was Ptah-Nouthor. The Great Hypostyle Hall was packed. The crowd was estimated at twenty thousand people, three quarters of whom were packed outside due to lack of space. But the acoustics were excellent, and each of the An-Nu's words stood out clearly without any particular vocal effort on his part. The Ahâ had been carried on his chair by eight first-class priests to the ebony and gold armchair which was only used for the passage of an Elder of direct blood.

This homily has been preserved thanks to funerary inscriptions. It is exemplary:

- You are the undisputed Master, O Meri-Ra, of our two "Hearts". The Elder, Ahâ-Men-Ptah, you watch over the sleep of the Blessed, bringing about on Earth the harmony desired by Heaven. You also command the destinies of the Parcels of our Second Heart, born of the First conceived by the Goddess Nut and her Earth-born husband Geb. You will be eternally alive, because you are also the Beloved of Ra, who spreads his blessings over your shoulders, making you invulnerable to the enemies of Ptah the One.

During this long sentence, Pepi remained motionless, like the statues representing him that can be admired in several museums. And this is how the Pontiff Ptah-Nouthor ended his homily:

- You are the undisputed Master, O Meri-ra, of our two Hearts. You are the Lord of the Two Mansions, earthly and heavenly, for you are the Beloved of the Divine Triad. You are also Pepi, Priest and Servant of Hator in the Temple of Ptah-Nut-Ra, as a descendant of Nut and Geb. These will be your divine and human Names from this day forward. They will be engraved everywhere and will form part of your royal seal. To you, O Pepi, eternal Life, Strength and Health.

All the priests bowed respectfully, while the crowd of faithful hurried towards the monumental double door to form a guard of honour and give the Ahâ Pépi a standing ovation. Meanwhile, the eight bearers in their long white robes, insignia of their rank in the priesthood, lifted the heavy chair and placed it on their shoulders, without the Lord of the Two Demons, Son of Heaven and Eternity, being able to detect a single jolt.

Only the Pontiff remained behind, to enter the secret doorway in the west-facing colonnade and make his way to the underground passageways leading to the entrance of the Golden Circle. It was in the Hall of Rest that the Masters of Measurement and Number would meet him to discuss the teaching to be given to the next class of novices, those who would form the future High Priests. Ptah-Nouthor fell into deep meditation. When he opened his eyes again, he saw around thirty shaven heads, topped by bodies lying on the ground. The Masters of Measurement and Number, who had arrived silently, had entered into communion with the Soul-Mother of Heaven, waiting for the Pontiff to complete his own dialogue with his Kâ.

As soon as he straightened up, the priests did the same in a single movement, rustling their long robes. With a slight smile, the An-Nu gestured broadly towards the black granite benches at the back of the room:

- Let's sit down, because if I've asked you to assist me today, it's because an important decision has to be made about a change to be made in one of the symbols of the Golden Circle, and therefore in the way it's taught to novices.

The Pontiff took a deep breath, while the Masters stared at him more closely:

- I'm referring to the 'Heart' that pulsates within the Cluster of the Fixed, which comes after the Cluster of the Lion. It followed the steady progress of the Cadets of the Survivors of our first sunken homeland, after they landed in Ta Mana[53], the Land of the Sunset. The symbol chosen during this distant period was the Scarab. It corresponded well to the image of a holy life, pulsating with potential for the new arrivals. It was also a fitting name for the Cadets, sons of our glorious Elders, those who had overcome the difficulties created by the Sons of the Sun. What's more, this Scarab[54] linked the Celestial Bull to earthly life. And here we are, a few solar revolutions away from the end of the Year of God, concluding the advent of our first Pêr-Ahâ, the Unifier Mêna, as foreseen. It's time to prepare the harmonisation of heaven with the advancement of our people to the "Second Heart". The Celestial Bull, by becoming the invisible and supreme ruler of the sunken Ahâ-Men-Ptah, also becomes the ruler of our Souls, whose fabric he shapes through the intermediary of the Twelve, predetermining them according to the Law of the Father in the Divine-Mathematical Combinations. It would therefore be misunderstood if his symbol were to remain precisely one of these Twelve!

Leaving a silence to allow his listeners to express their opinions, the Pontiff took the opportunity to display for all to see a map of the heavens that had been rolled up at his feet. It was a multicoloured copy of the map of the heavens that had represented the locations of the Wanderers and the Fixed on the day of the Great Cataclysm. He continued, with everyone waiting for the next part without asking questions:

- In Ahâ-Men-Ptah, the Scarab symbolised the Golden Circle, since it was the pole of attraction for the Twelve gathered around the Sun. The iconography of the Sacred Barks, which fulfilled their function by saving the Elders and those who had accompanied them, has been perpetuated to this day. Nevertheless, if in our Holy

---

[53] Ta Mana has become Morocco, but in Arabic it still means the "Setting Place": Moghreb-el-Aqsa.

[54] A type of beetle is still known in Latin as the "Flying Bull".

Language we keep the sign for the engraving, we will change it symbolically. Do any of you have any suggestions?

This question deserved an answer, but no one spoke up here either. Probably because everyone knew that the Pontiff had already given a great deal of thought to this question, to which he had the answer! So Ptah-Nouthor continued:

- I know that our imagination has already made it possible to reconstruct the whole of Knowledge in its minutest detail. But this image is distorted, alas, according to each person's temperament. So I cannot rely on the impressions left by the texts to strengthen and reinforce the teaching of the Commandments. They are imposed on us by the stretched spiral, not the perfect circle, of the Divine Creature. We must therefore follow this eternal combinatory movement, without failing by the length of an inch to its geometric form and mathematical formulations. In this way, we will not run the risk of shaping God in our image, and only the opposite will remain valid. Because little by little, it seems that even in the preaching of our priests, the modelling of creatures by the Almighty Creator is being forgotten! What should be forgotten by all the Servants of the Creator is that they are human beings! Only a Creature endowed with a Divine Particle is capable of receiving the manifestation of the celestial emanations of the Twelve, without the help of the human senses which perceive and distort sounds and images! Now, both are capable of being double, that is to say, true or false, good or bad. Since God is the Reason of the Universe, he was the Word before the Word. He clothed sounds with holy and particular Names before attributing forms to each thing to express his will reasonably and humanly. The Scarab was this image of the Divine Word, uniting it with universal Reason made flesh in humanity. The Scarab covered a whole, since it sponsored all twelve at once! Those of Usir and those of Set were guaranteed protection until their unification, which took place, as the Divine-Mathematical Combinations intended, under the reign of Mena, the first Elder on this earth. As the Year of God draws to a close, it's time to turn the page.

Pointing with an outstretched index finger to the map of the sky spread out at his feet, the Pontiff continued, bending down towards a precise point:

- The cluster of Scarab Fixes has the characteristic shape of certain hard-bodied sea animals. And if our 'Flying Bull' fits in well with the Twelve, one of these beasts would give total continuity to the whole of this figuration, which has changed its meaning since the Great Cataclysm. It's a fish that moves backwards in order to walk! It seems that the Creator, in creating this specimen, indicated it to us in this way to make his choice clear! For this is the Scarab, which was the first symbol of the Renaissance, but which, because of the inversion of the "Belt of Twelve", has become the last. The Crab, since it is the Crab and its backward march, will clearly indicate the phenomenon of this reversal of the Universe in relation to the Earth, which occurred on the date indicated on this celestial map. The warning will thus be heard and understood by all the generations that will follow us in the centuries and millennia that will perpetuate the future. Note the incredible intelligence of your predecessors, the Masters of Measurement and Number, who, in drawing the Belt, made it in the form of a spiral with the last sign, the Scarab, just above Leo, thus allowing the change we are making today by calling it the Crab. What's more, if another important event occurs later, this will allow your Cadets to give it yet another Name without there being a break in harmonisation with the rest[55]. Only intangibility in permanent evolution and according to the One Law instituted at the Beginning, must guide our pursuit of the teaching of Mathematical Combinations. This is how our Elders made the beginning of the Year of God coincide with the enthronement of the unifying Pêr-Ahâ Mêna. And so, for the start of another Sep'ti year[56]. We must be ready to move the Golden

---

[55] The break came a millennium and a half later with the end of the Middle Kingdom. The Masters of the time called this constellation "CANCER", as well as the parallel that served as a guideline for the Survivors to reach their second land promised by Ptah.

[56] Remember that this Year of God lasted 1,461 years.

Circle in the direction of the Earth's march through Space. This inauguration of the "Crab" Fixes will take place on the first day of Teta in year one of the second revolution of the star dedicated to our good Hathor. This will be the greatest celebration of the near future, which we will have to announce in all the provinces of the 'Second Heart', while the servant of our Good Mother Hathor, the divine Pépi, prepares the official festivities as soon as he arrives in the capital. For the Golden Circle, the Crab of Twelve will keep the same celestial dimension: twenty-six parts of the Belt of 360. As a result, the influence will not change in any way, nor will the value of the terms of the five Wanderers crossing this Fix. So: for the one closest to Ra, Hor-Septa[57], which glorifies the benevolence of Ptah on the day of the Sun-Sep'ti conjunction that saved Horus from disaster, a domination of the first six parts; for the next: Hor-Hen-Nout[58], which glorifies maternal love and Hor's rescue, an identical domination of six parts provides the best combinations in this fixed point; the third is the bloody Hor-Py-Tesch. This Red Wanderer, whose name glorifies Hor's valour, will only ever dominate the next five games. The fourth is Hor-Cheta, whose long-lasting beneficial effects during the Rebirth of the Survivors will be the best of all, even if she only lasts five games. Then there is Hor-Sar-Kher, in fifth and last place, with the last four parts of the twenty-six, who is only known for his evil deeds in this place, as you already know. Since there is nothing to change either in the combinatorial prediction of general events to come, let us turn to the particular signs of the various human groups born during Ra's passage through this cluster, or transiting through it at a primordial moment of earthly life. Your attention has already been drawn to the noticeable changes in both the movements and their effects. They are shifted precisely by the retreat of the Twelve from the Earth, which changes the meaning of the Mathematical Combinations, if not their forms. For, even if this has become simple routine for us,

---

[57] The details of the following passage can be found in chapter VI of this book. The planet is Mercury.

[58] The planet, or Errant, is Venus. The next planets are: Mars, Jupiter and Saturn, the most distant.

never forget that the cause of human events is influenced by the movement of the Wanderers in relation to the combinatorial positions of the Twelve, assisted in the order willed by God, by the Sun and the Moon. And we should remember even more strongly that these causes are willed by God and that his will is stronger than ours combined for the great problems that he often solves in his own way. It is the application of this heavenly Commandment that we must understand and apply as a priority, even if it seems contrary to what we might be tempted to advocate. And the beginning of the action we will be able to undertake will not depend in any way on secondary conditions, but on the sole will of the Divine-Mathematical Combinations. It is therefore necessary to know very precisely the birth movement of each human being whose earthly life will be taken into consideration. In this, there is no hesitation to be had, since the Name, this human name necessary for the camel envelope to be in spirit power, can only be given to it when the cord linking the mother to the baby is cut. It is at this precise moment that the brain is struck by the influxes of the Twelve, which impregnate the cortex hard and indelibly with a predetermination that will lead its actions according to the divine will if its upbringing is done properly. The Pêr-Ahâ are always born at the right moment, in the Leo cluster, conception being monitored so that it occurs at the right moment for childbirth. We have sometimes performed Caesarean sections when there was a delay, so that God would still bless the birth with the most beneficial influences, so that the astral positions would condition the Elder as God wishes in his celestial configurations. The germ received from the man by the woman conditions only the body, the envelope of the future human. But as long as the Divine Parcel has not made contact with the body, the being has no Name: it is only a little something, in the same way as a chicken or a lamb that we taste during a meal. But that certainly doesn't mean that you can kill a little man with impunity. Its seed has also been given by God, so that the one who will become a full-fledged creature from birth may germinate and be born. He alone should have the right to life or death over the camel that is not yet human. We have always preached that it is forbidden to kill one's neighbour, since this axiom is a divine commandment. Its transgression would bring back all the misfortunes that befell some and others during the fighting between the two fratricidal clans. But to return to the time of the Cadets, and their births, the babies will not take on their Name of Man until after childbirth, when the body is separated from that of the mother, and the head is impregnated with the influence of the Twelve. Conception, being unknown to the celestial combinations, must likewise be unknown to us. Conception is not the beginning of human life, although a heart beats. There is indeed the same carnal element in the goose that we enjoy at our meals! Only the soul counts, and that is the gift that Ptah gives us to obey his Law, and his Law alone!

With a sigh, and letting his arms strike against his body, the Pontiff nodded before continuing:

- I have often enough developed the twofold aspect of the popular mind, which too easily allows itself to be manoeuvred into its misfortunes by subversive idolatrous theories, to return to it again here. But your responsibility in teaching novices is such that it is incumbent upon you to be fully and completely aware of your role as educator. To discern the true from the false, when a dispute arises in your Divine Parcel, a profound meditation is necessary between it and God. From this will spring the spark that will grant you the Word in harmony with the Word of the Sacred Texts, the unique basis of our theology. Under no circumstances should your personal judgement of past or future events interfere with the teaching you receive. As for me, I have made it a habit, from my earliest youth, not to give the slightest place to anything that might appear to me as a complementary light to what has been written by those who were simply relating the Truth, because they lived it. Which is not to say that you should deny your own personality and its inner hearing, which may assail you with its voices. But you mustn't let them overwhelm you unthinkingly. You must give your ideas time to develop within you and to become perfected, because they will undergo the transformations that dialogue with the omnipresent Great Shaper of all things, even the most impalpable, inevitably brings. He will remove what is insignificant and unnecessary, and develop what deserves to be developed. And then you will agree that your teaching will shine with the double brilliance of Truth and Light. This must be your path, as it will be for those who will be your pupils throughout your time in the

Golden Circle in this constellation of the Crab, successor to the Scarab, and awaiting another definition in two millennia' time by my distant successor. It will be the sign of the power of the Twelve, coming directly from heaven to indicate its retreat and divine omnipotence. His Triad will remain eternally the justification for this, for as Ptah created the heavens, so he modelled the earth, and made all the things that exist on it, before begetting the creature in his image. Always keep before your eyes this notion, invisible yet palpable at every moment, that in the Creator's Creation there is a Law *willed, prepared and meditated before being conceived in a length of time that is beyond our comprehension and yet not equal to a second of Eternity.*

After beating his chest three times, Ptah Nouthor, despite his great age, straightened up, before continuing in an even more energetic voice:

- This is why my conclusion today will be somewhat prophetic, because it is after a long meditation that I deliver it to you. Our carnal envelope has no existence, no reason to exist on Earth, except through the animation that is breathed into it by the Divine Parcel. It took millions and millions of revolutions of the Wandering Ones, and as many evolutions of the Fixed Ones, for a certain body to take on its human form. Then other millions of years for the shaping of souls to reach our Time. What proves the reality of the facts is that the foundation of the Parcels provided by the Twelve is the same for all humanity, whether they have white, black or red skin. It is this aspect of the Law of Creation that differentiates man from beast, despite the animal's power to emit sounds and therefore to speak. We are the only beings to possess a close link with the Eternal. We must therefore not only be grateful to him, but also make ourselves his faithful servants and defenders, preserving intact the Knowledge that he has transmitted to us so that we can continually rise towards him. The idolaters must not distort the original theology for their own benefit. For, having come into possession of this Sacred Knowledge, they would then reign as undisputed masters. You will always have to try and find, behind each new pupil, the one who will eventually be the pestiferous sheep. Stemming from Set, whose envy and jealousy have been perpetuated through the millennia, the rebellious Sun worshippers who have not understood that holy union is the only way to survive and develop will always try to ensure a supremacy that can only lead to a new cataclysm, or the pure and simple end of our Second Heart. Glory be to our God, the One! As long as we respect him and keep him in our minds, in all his purity, our second homeland will live on. I have finished; may the Lord continue to watch over us all, inspiring us in our future work.

The reign of Pepi I[er] lasted fifty-three years, during which time the Pontiff was able to make a useful contribution by re-establishing absolute integrity in dogma. However, H died too quickly to allow for a smooth succession, since his only son was only seven years old when he died. It was therefore the Queen Mother who held the de facto Spectrum, but it was the Grand Vizier who held the power. His name was Ouni, and he had been Governor of the Southern Provinces. It was he who had it written on the walls of his tomb "that he administered the country with such firmness and justice that not a single village or family under his equitable jurisdiction quarrelled with its neighbours or lacked anything".

But the concern of this Ouni was to increase productivity in all categories of quarries supplying the hundreds of gigantic works in progress. He even went as far as the Last Cataract in Nubia to open a new centre for extracting granite blocks, which were soon decorating buildings as far away as those in the Nile delta.

He was succeeded by Khouf-Hor, a native of Elephantine who dreamt of taking revenge on those who had frustrated his ancestors. He became famous for the four expeditions he organised to the farthest reaches of the Empire. It was during the third, to Nubia, that Méri-En-Râ, the thirteen-year-old Pêr-Ahâ he had taken with him, died of a "fever". He was embalmed on the way back to Men-Nefer (Memphis) and buried in his own tomb. It was found there just over a century ago in a perfectly preserved state.

The Queen Mother, who was still alive, passed on the Sceptre to her younger brother, who was only six years old at the time, under the royal name of: Nefer-Kâ-Râ, or more commonly Pepi II.

And Khuf-Hor, although he had other views, could only keep his position as Grand Vizier.

Curiously, this reign lasted a century! It ended in total anarchy, because this Sceptre, held endlessly by a willful but senile old man, put the whole country in a state of rebellion. Thus ended, in complete confusion, the dynasty that Manetho called the Sixth.

Chapter XI

PERPETUAL ANTAGONISM
(THE GEMINI CONSTELLATION)

> *"We know, for example, that from remote antiquity monotheism was the occult doctrine of the priests of Osiris, and that polytheism and myths were no more than a shiny cloth designed to veil the people in the philosophical truths that would have made them strong.*
>
> S. KARPPE
> *(The origins of the Zohar.)*

> *"I can see that the weeds are choking off the good wheat,*
> *And my mind is not so thick, nor so troubled*
> *That I do not feel that the first Church,*
> *By the passage of time, has lost much of the light!"*
>
> PIERRE DE RONSARD
> *(Profession of Faith, 1563).*

It happened, as had been foreseen for centuries, that in this Second Heart of God, blessed by the Eternal, there was no longer any Pêr-Ahâ powerful enough to rule. At that time, there was also a king who reigned over the Delta provinces, and he was a Hycksos invader: an "Immonde"!

We are in the shifting terrain of the fifteenth and sixteenth dynasties, which counted a good forty holders of the Sceptre, some of whom had to share their sovereignty with a usurper. This was the case with Ahâ Apêpi, who wished to take back the south of the country under his authority, which was under the domination of a Sun-worshipper who had made a city further north of Dendera his fiefdom, which would later become the opulent Thebes of the Hundred Golden Gates.

As the forces of the two clans were more or less equal, Ahâ Apêpi needed a reasonable reason to try once again for unification without the Followers of Horus losing what was left to them!

A pretext for this was provided by the Pontiff of Denderah, whose religious edifice had not been destroyed, but into which no one could enter to pray to the Good Mother Nut on pain of the worst evils. And the good people, listening to the reasons of the Sun worshippers, and finally accepting them, went to worship the Virgin Queen in the temples built by the impious Rebels who argued that Nut had given birth to Set, in order to achieve this goal.

Now, since the hippopotamus was the iconographic symbol of the figurative representation of Ptah, these peaceful animals were being hunted down relentlessly in all the rivers and lakes in the south of the country, in order to destroy them! This was the subject of the desperate appeal by the Pontiff of Dendera to the Pêr-Ahâ, the only legal representative of divine power in his eyes. This, of course, King Apêpi could not accept. So he sent a special courier to the Hyksos Seken-En-Râ with an ultimatum, which the latter rejected.

A merciless war took place at the outposts of Thebes, and the "Immonde" (as he is called in the Tentyrite texts) was savagely killed by those avenging the hundreds of hippopotamuses cowardly murdered by Set's descendants.

The mummy of this Hycksos, also found intact, if we can call this envelope covered in strips intact! The head was terrifyingly deformed by the wounds. The forehead, split by an axe, showed a hole several centimetres long, full of hair and blood. Another blow from a blade pierced the brain through the right eye. It's likely that this "royal" rebel wasn't quite dead yet, as several other blows struck him, including two post-mortem ones: a sword blow entered the left side of his head, just above the ear, as well as a mace blow that crushed his nose! Hycksos undoubtedly suffered the effects of the hatred he had engendered among those who venerated the hippopotamus as the earthly representation of Ptah the One. The face has undoubtedly been tortured to the extreme. The mummy's teeth are still clamped down on the tongue, which they bite deeply, and the convulsively clenched hands show perfectly the terrible suffering he underwent before giving up the ghost!

Although Denderah was returned to its cult, the usurpers continued to reign further south. It was not until a century later that unification was achieved once again, but only for a short time. Such was the antagonism between the two fratricidal clans that lasting peace now seemed impossible between the cadets, even though they were descended from the same, unique Mother!

But what interests us here is the resumption of the cult of Ptah in the third reconstruction of the original temple, on the same sacred site. The Ahâ Apêpi has restored all his powers to the An-

Nu Psên-Hapy[59], who thus becomes once again the Pontiff of the College of High Priests, and the unchanging rhythm of the initiatory meetings, instead of taking place solely in the shadow of the subterranean halls of the Golden Circle, can resume in the teaching halls of the Great Temple, under the protection of the graceful smile of Nut, or of her daughter Iset, who blooms at the top of the twenty-four pillars of the Hypostyle Hall.

The first free meeting thus took place after more than a century of total eclipse. Underneath his debonair exterior, the Pontiff was even more sombre and pessimistic than he had wished. The future hardly looked bright to him, despite the apparent signs of victory in the present. The joyful hubbub of the priests seated in front of him did not inspire him.

So he raised his face towards the shaven heads, indicating with an outstretched hand that he was about to speak. Silence fell quickly, allowing him to speak without raising his voice:

- We are back in the Temple, and we thank God for it! But we mustn't shout our joy too loudly, because there is no doubt that we are cursed and will remain so until we are gone for good!

The dismayed looks on the faces of the monks showed their incomprehension at the words of their revered leader, who had given them so much support during the long period of darkness and opprobrium. Psên-Hapy explained without further ado:

- It is more than two centuries since the constellation Aries added Ra to its circle of influence on Earth. The Celestial Bull, blessed be he eternally, has returned to the darkness of the Kingdom of the Sleeping Ones for a very long time. The Sun therefore remains at the sole disposal of its idolaters, and woe betide us! I say it aloud, and this warning will come true: the

---

[59] This name of High Priest was used several times by Greek authors, without it being clear why, under the phonetisation of Psenophis. In hieroglyphic, it means: "The Pilot of the Celestial River".

perpetual antagonism between Ptah and Ra has begun a new process of annihilation of our second homeland! The Pêr-Ahâ has defeated the Immonde who was killing all: the earthly representations of our God. Glory to him for the justice he has done us! For the hippopotamus, as big as it is, and so horrible to look at that you turn your head away so as not to shiver with fear, is the gentlest and most peaceful animal there is. It doesn't even eat meat, which is not the case with us! So the Immonde has been wiped out, but his brother is already regaining power further south! Ra will favour him, because his navigation is beneficial to him. The influence of their scurrilous worshippers, who preach the primacy of the Sun, is already growing. These cursed worshippers are building a new metropolis for the advent of an idolatry symbolised by a long avenue of gigantic statues with ram heads[60]. It will be our necropolis, for we shall never rise again!

A disapproving murmur went round the assembly of priests who, all too happy to be out in the fibre air, wanted to keep their eyes closed to the reality the Pontiff was describing to them. The old Patriarch smiled bitterly, before repeating in a disillusioned tone:

- All this will obviously not happen in our lifetime on earth, or even that of our children or grandchildren, but it will happen before Ra's navigation of the Aries cluster is completed. Before putting the circle of celestial configurations in order, it seems necessary to remind you of our human antecedents. Faithful to the tradition of our Elders, those who populated Ahâ-Men-Ptah as Creatures of God, my thoughts have always been turned towards uprightness and obedient behaviour in the application of the Commandments of the Law of Creation issued by Usir at the instigation of his Father: the Supreme Creator. You all know as well as I do that human nature, especially when it is doubly distributed, is marred by a great weakness. Over the millennia, this has led to bloody battles

---

[60] This is the triumphal way from Thebes to Luxor, which was just over eight kilometres long and featured giant statues of rams every fifty metres on either side of the road.

and fierce hatred between two clans, even though they are members of the same family. And in the rare moments of appeasement, the annals speak only of fatal passions, perverse jealousies and shameful scheming. This incessant antagonism could only fan the flames of a new divine wrath! It is ready to be unleashed and there is nothing more we can do about it, except try to save what can still be saved, as my predecessors did with our sunken Elder Heart. The people have neglected their elementary duty towards their almighty Modeller, by abandoning their thanksgiving to him, in favour of blasphemous and idolatrous worship of the sun! This iniquitous failure to give basic thanks to God's goodness, his protector as well as his benefactor, can only result in exemplary punishment for all, not only for the people, but also for ourselves, who not believe in God enough to make up for human weakness and have his rule imposed upon us. This formulation, so luminous for us who had at our disposal the four elements implying total mastery of the Parcels in order to ensure their salvation, we let it slip away! It has been hijacked and distorted by the Immondes! And the rebellious souls are going to suffer all the horrible contingencies of this inhospitable earth, before leaving their carnal envelopes and continuing their eternal wandering in an uncertain elsewhere. A hypocritical mysticism has manifested itself among the rebels since the Sun entered Aries. The animal intelligence of their leaders has successfully tried to combat their own divine origin, despite coming from their ancestor Set. We, for our part, have endeavoured to combat the evil brought about by this idolatrous faction. This often forced us to question our faith, and that was fine as long as we felt the spark of the Bull pulsating within us on our behalf! This Good was characterised by a notion of love surrounding all beings; and this Good no longer exists today! This may seem strange to our minds, which are just emerging from the darkness of the underground. We have become accustomed to the rigorous control of all our celestial mathematics, to its logical and precise concatenation, so that we fail to recognise that we will have to wipe the slate clean of all our knowledge if novices no longer come here, but continue to go to the Zoology buildings dedicated to the ram, supposedly more in tune with the Sun, the source of the light illuminating the ground but not of the celestial Light, the source of nourishment for our souls. Our successors will die the most atrocious death at the hands of those who will then die a definitive death because their Divine Parcels will rot within them! Our souls are placed too high by the Creator, blessed be He forever, whatever may happen to us, for us not to do everything in our power in the short time of this present moment, so that even the Immondes understand their values. Let us therefore remove from the engravings of our Golden Circle the representation of the two antagonists who were Ousir and Ousit through the unique fault of the latter, who took the name of Sit[61] in order to defy his divine brother for all eternity. In the first 'Heart', this cluster of Twelve was represented by two lotus flowers from the same root. We will repeat this engraving, but with the symbolic name of "Twins". For the younger generations, we must erase from our Annals this hatred that has persisted through the millennia. Let us take advantage of the fact that we are once again in a position of strength to show mercy and forgetfulness towards those who were our brothers before becoming our enemies.

A murmur of approval followed this diatribe, despite some disapproving whispers. The Pontiff's irritation was quickly suppressed in the face of this obvious challenge to a state of affairs that could only bring survival to all, rather than general annihilation. Nevertheless, he continued in a measured voice:

- I'm going to remind you how the Divine Word, the Soul of souls, created our understanding and our intelligence within the events that surround us. This is what constitutes our mysticism, our unconditional agreement in the Great Work of the Eternal. In the beginning, God created the heavens; and before placing the earth in its proper place, he surrounded it with a belt of pure crystalline forces. With our terrestrial globe at the centre, as time went by, and according to the mathematical formulae that you have studied at length, the Creator filled it with the most unusual plants and animals, but vital for the future of his ultimate creation: the carnal envelope destined to receive a particle of the Soul-One. And the

---

[61] Read *Le Grand Cataclysme*, a detailed account of the lives of these two half-brothers, Usir and Usit.

radiations of the Twelve arriving on Earth from all sides at once were united, interwoven with each other after having reverberated through the Wanderers before arriving on Earth to await a body to irradiate for the life of a fundamental canvas that would thus link it to its Creator. Whether we like it or not, we are linked to him in an indissoluble way with no possibility of rebellion, something the idolaters do not understand, and which they have never wanted to admit by denying the divine birthright to Usir. This is why those who rebel against the Law will not have access to the Kingdom of the Blessed. They will not have Eternity to sing the praises of what they have hated all their earthly lives. Which is very little consolation, because the eternal return of souls to the bosom of the cosmic Whole is the logical sequence of the continuous movement that animates all Creation as it advances through Time and Space. Every new birth of a carnal envelope provokes the penetration of influxes injected into a Particle of the Creator Soul, which thus returns to Earth. Death does not exist for the human soul if it has demonstrated purity and obedience to the precepts that have enabled it to become what it is. God created the sea and the rivers that flow into it. And yet, for millions and millions of years, the sea has never overflowed! So we have to admit that there is room, not only for all our Divine Parcels in the Elysian Fields of Amenta, but also for the souls of the Immodest if we can manage to make ourselves understood by them and instil in them what we consider to be the One and Only elementary Truth: the Primacy of God over our actions. If we fail in this ultimate effort at union, it seems that there is no further recourse to expect from the creative mechanism. Even if we scrutinise the geometrical configurations of mathematical combinations with the eyes of the soul, there is no chance, not even a secondary one, of making the evolutionary spiral evolve towards any kind of improvement. It diverts our humanity from the direct path and draws us towards a centre that can only determine a bottomless abyss! No longer on our small human dimension but on that of Eternity, we will be plunged into a frightening abyss that will have no end! That's why I insist so much on the cosmic understanding of your intellects in the absence of an all-too-human oblivion of the past. The sign of the Twins must personify this last attempt at harmonious understanding with the One who created us all. After all, look our monotheism in the face, as I do: it's not that far removed from the solar idolatry of our blood brothers!

Lightning striking in the middle of this venerable assembly of priests could not have turned them into better statues! The shaven heads didn't dare move. Their private thoughts showed through their eyes as if they had been spoken: "Has the Pontiff suddenly gone mad? Had their ears heard such blasphemy? And despite the seriousness of the situation, the An-Nu could not hold back a smile as he said:

- Our monotheism is, in short, the great Dogma handed down to us by our Elders. It is the essence of the Message of Usir. It is therefore not so far removed from the zoolatry in use among those of Set, although at first sight we are well aware of the imitative sacrilege of the Rebels to the Law. What will happen in the future, when our two peoples have disappeared because they failed to unite, and barbarians living in other lands try to explain our religion and the reasons for our discord? It will not be difficult for them to see all the similarities, because the same divine spirit was involved in both cases at the outset! Already, in our ancient writings, our predecessors adopted a certain form of polytheism in an attempt to keep the people in line with the paths laid out by the Almighty. To inspire fear of God, and then fear of exemplary punishment, they created assessors responsible for moral supervision. As for us, who for two millennia have never ceased to affirm that we are on this blessed soil of heaven, that the Eternal One has created everything under His sole Name, that no human being can equal Him, and that outside His omnipotence there is nothing but nothingness, we have accepted the proliferation of a host of idols in order to satisfy the thirst of humans to want to believe only in "heavenly" signs!... Shame on us for accepting such an outrage! The blessed name of Nut was no longer enough to attract the crowds, so we substituted that of her daughter Iset, blessed be she eternally, for it is not her sanctity that is in question, but ours. And then, as one cycle came to an end, Iset seemed to return this temple dedicated to the Lady of Heaven to oblivion; so, as there was no longer a valid 'goddess', she was transformed into ten thousand scattered names! In this case, it was Hathor, who reflected her role as the mother of Horus.

But from that day on, the good Virgin Queen Nut was doomed to oblivion! The entire universe, God's creation, underwent just as many transformations in the writings of other temples. The Divine Potter has lost the clay needed for his modelling! Shame on us, and beware of us all! We are no longer creatures of the Creator. Under the pretext of making our monotheism more popular, we have not hesitated to resort to a colourful language, full of subversive metaphors, imbued in content and form with the purest polytheism. And if today we ourselves are in a compromise between our monotheism and idolatry, the zoologists of the solar ram are trying to transform it into a sacrilegious monotheism. The original divine element from our venerated forefathers disappears. The Supreme Being cannot but be very irritated by this. The irremediable is happening all over again. Let's try to save what we can outside our borders, because there won't be a stone left standing in our "Second Heart". Unless the sand submerges our temples and their superstructures, such as the Golden Circle, and some day in the distant future, Cadets from another nation visiting our soil make the discovery.

The appalled looks on the faces of the priests clearly showed how suddenly they had realised the prophetic value of what would sooner or later become the grim reality. The Pontiff continued in a less overwhelmed tone:

- In my opinion, our monotheism, although no longer part of divine grace, can nevertheless be preserved in its past integrity. The Golden Circle is the materiality of the Law of Creation, and it is in it that we must place the safeguard of the Sacred Writings. The structure of the universe and the mechanism of the cogs that compose it amply demonstrate the indisputable authority of the Creator over all things and all beings. Our spirit must therefore tend to make both our enemy brothers and the two younger brothers of the future understand that the fundamental principles of Usir and Usit were the same, since they emanated from God through Nut. Our efforts will henceforth consist in replacing the sky on our maps and astral representations *in* the opposite direction, *at the antipode*, to what it has been since the Great Cataclysm. We will re-establish the old figuration in such a way as to show God that we are escaping from this time, that our souls are externalising themselves, escaping from themselves so that they are no longer constrained to follow a predetermination due to Reason alone. Having restored a very fragile balance in this way, I agree, we may perhaps triumph on the perilous path of retransmitting the Holy Text, beyond our return to the Land of the Blessed Sleeping Ones. May Ptah, in his infinite goodness, forgive those who came before us for choosing the hippopotamus as an image of the One. The hippopotamus did not represent a form of zoolatry similar to the solar cult of the rebels, but the symbol of celestial peace in a form that could inspire human fear. This animal has almost completely disappeared from our lands because of blind vengeance, but we are responsible for its disappearance because we agreed to perpetuate this idolatrous cult. May this conclusion not be the end of our civilisation, but a springboard to a future that is far more understanding of God's desires for us.

Psên-Hapy had ended his harangue in the tone of a normal conversation, not wishing to prophesy too much. But the Pontiff knew that he had spoken with the voice and words of Truth. He certainly wouldn't see the end of their world, but the end of the Sun's passage through this constellation of Aries would already be lighting up nothing but ruins!

None of the priests dared to stand up until the venerable Patriarch was on his feet, so he sighed in resignation and said as he rose:

- It's time to make models of our new Twins. Let's go up to the observatory and get to work.

Twenty-four Pêr-Ahâ succeeded this Apêpi, whom the Greeks called Apophis, driving the country a little further into chaos with each new Sceptre. But the bottom had been reached. Decadence had become such that it could no longer increase. So the time of the twenty-fifth Pêr-Ahâ was the time of an attempt at renewal and unification. He took the name of Nek-Bet Iâmet, he who was born of the Greek Nephtys, i.e. the Moon. In this way, he was sure not to offend either the worshippers of the Sun or the Followers of

Horus! His wife was Nefertari, whose splendid tomb can be found in the Valley of the Queens, and who should not be confused with the beautiful Nefertiti, wife of Akhenaten two centuries later.

Pharaoh and his troops laid siege to Avaris, in the delta, where the Hycksos, who had ruled part of the country for several centuries, had entrenched themselves. They finally surrendered on the express condition that they be allowed to leave the banks of the Nile and go to northern Judah, from whence they had come. But as they continued to pose a serious threat to Egypt, the king attacked them at Sharouben, and captured the city after a siege that lasted three years.

This period, which marks the beginning of the New Kingdom according to the most famous historian of Antiquity, Manetho, and which there is no reason to doubt, was also the starting point of what Jewish tradition calls the oppression of the Hebrew people in Egypt, which lasted two hundred and forty years. The date of the biblical Exodus can therefore be found precisely, and therefore under the reign in which it took place. As this study is the subject of a forthcoming volume in this series, it will not be discussed here.

With this reign, all the ancient traditions were re-established, in particular the matriarchal system. It was for this reason that Queen Nefertari was venerated, after her death, as the divine grandmother and mother of this 23rd dynasty.

The Pêr-Ahâ who succeeded him was Djezer-Kâ-Râ-Amonhotep, who was, as his name suggests, a worshipper of the Sun in Aries, and the founder of an important lineage that went all the way back to Amenophis IV, who renounced Amun and the Sun in favour of Aten and Ptah, under the name of Akhenaten. But what we do know about this Immonde was that he had temples rebuilt that had been destroyed during the 13th dynasty and dedicated to Ra! What's more, he had a splendid temple erected to ensure the worship of his spirit after his death. Today, this edifice forms an integral part of the group of buildings known as Médinet-Habou, at the southern end of the Thebes necropolis.

He was succeeded by a "Son of Teta", or of Thoth to the Greeks, who was given the name Thuthmosis Ier by Manetho. As a worthy Pêr-Ahâ, he devoted the thirteen years of his reign to turning Egypt back into a country worthy of its ancestral tradition. Not only did he undertake immense works, but he also waged several successful military campaigns. Just above the third cataract, a border marker bore the following inscription:

"Glory to Djou-T-Atêta, long life and eternal health to him who deposed the chief of the Nubians and holds his people in his hands! He has returned to his ancient borders on both banks of the Great River, and there is not a frizzy-haired man left who dares attack him, for none would survive, all the others having died in the battle. They fell by the sword, and they litter the ground with their rotting flesh! These carcasses are too numerous for the vau tours to leave nothing but bones on the ground. Henceforth, no one will cross this spot without being authorised to do so, because, like a panther in a herd of fleeing gazelles, the glory of the Son of Atêta dazzles them and prevents them from advancing! Notice to all!"

Two of the sons of Thuthmosis Ier had died very young, so the king had focused all his affection on his daughter, ignoring her fourth child, who was a boy, although we don't know exactly why. This daughter was the one who was to become so famous under the name of Hatshepsut! But it was much later, and after many setbacks.

As soon as the Pharaoh died, and according to tradition, his last son took over as second in line. But Hatshepsut, the eldest, aged fifteen and manipulated by supporters of Ptah, rebelled and declared that her father had always wanted her to be queen. In response, the priests of Amun, already in constant ascendance to the zenith of heaven, forced her to marry her brother and content herself with the thankless role of queen-consort!

The couple had a daughter, but the king soon turned his back on his wife and had a son by a concubine of non-royal blood. And shortly before the end of his reign, to prevent Hatschepsut from taking the Sceptre, the king arranged for this son to be plebiscited by the people with the approval of the priests of Amun. The queen was furiously angered... and Pêr-Ahâ was murdered! But the party of the supporters of Ptah was no longer strong enough, and it was the third king, Thutmose, who ascended the throne. Hatschepsut was appointed co-regent but had to keep her title of queen consort!

From the start of his reign, the young king found himself confined to a secondary role by his mother-in-law, who had clearly assumed power. According to tradition, he was prepared to marry his half-sister, but Hatschepsut would have none of it, as her daughter would then have become the legitimate heiress and the pharaoh would have regained the Sceptre!

For nine years, he succeeded in maintaining equal registration with the queen consort, but then abruptly disappeared from the political scene, although he lived for another thirteen years. Hatschepsut was crowned "King of the Two Lands". From that day on, she insisted on being called "King", not "Queen". Her destiny was such that her life will be the subject of a special book. For this reason, her reign will not be dealt with at length here.

The successors had fairly combative reigns on the fringes of their borders, but they all had to deal with perpetual internal antagonism from one clan or another, depending on whether they were worshippers of the Sun or followers of Horus!

Curiously, Egypt, which was invincible at the time, educated several hundred foreign princes at its court, but they were mainly used as hostages. And these young men had brought with them a kind of languor and voluptuousness that had spread in a few short years. And for the first time, during the short reign of Thutmose the Fourth, Egypt had to worry about political contingencies outside the Nile Valley.

So when he died, there was consternation, for Amonhotep, his son, was only eleven years old and had no sister to marry to establish his right to the throne. Nevertheless, he was made to marry a princess with many titles despite her thirteen years! She was named "Lady of the Two Lands", making her the legal heir to the throne.

And here again, the blatant antagonism appears throughout this reign, for while the weak Amenhotep III had fallen under the influence of Amun the Ram, this was not the case with Queen Tii, his young wife, who worshipped the One God!

Chapter XII

THE ADVENT OF ATON
(The Constellation of Aries)

> *"The Wanderers, those who never stop running, are only the visible reflections of the combinations of cosmic forces, but they do not emit any force of their own.*
>
> JUNCTIN
> *(Speculum Astrologiae.)*

> *"On the colossal buildings there were still Egyptian characters that recalled the ancient splendour of Thebes. Asked to translate, one of the old priests explained to Germanicus that the city had once had more than 700,000 inhabitants of warlike age."*
>
> TACITUS
> *(Annales, II, page 60).*

Thebes, the capital with a hundred golden gates dear to Homer, into which a hundred soldiers could enter abreast, was at the height of its glory. For centuries, every Pêr-Ahâ had had a temple built as much for his own glory as for that of Amon-Râ, the Solar Ram. And each time, the building eclipsed that of its predecessor in beauty, richness of decoration and imposing grandeur! The priests of the Sun worshippers were all powerful, and they firmly controlled the destiny of the "Second Heart" through Pharaoh, reduced to the role of a statue of God.

Not only had Denderah lost the members of its famous Double House of Life, but the general silting-up of the site had buried the Golden Circle under decades of oblivion. The last old priests had died there, isolated in their defunct monotheism! And yet no, because from Heliopolis, the city of the Sun, the primitive An, an evolution had taken place to counteract the predominance of Ouaset, the "Western City of Set", which became Thebes in Greek!

It was even more than an evolution: it was a spiritual revolution! The priests of this capital dedicated to the Sun God transformed it into a new cult: that of a divinity acting through the intermediary of the Sun. Unable to give it the name of Ptah, which had fallen into disuse, they anaglyphised the characters to transform them into Aten, as opposed to Amun, which served no ancient ideology!

In fact, the priests of Amun in Thebes amassed immense fortunes and lived lavishly without worrying about any theology other than making everyone obey them for their own well-being! Despite their primitive idolatry, the people of Heliopolis, and with them all the 'Rebels of Set', worshipped the Sun only in open opposition to the Followers of Horus. The transformation of Ra into Aten was therefore the primordial schism of the years preceding the reign of Amenophis III, and it is vital to know about it because it is vital to the historical understanding of the rest of the Annals of Ath-Kà-Ptah.

The Pêr-Ahâ, enthroned under his name Amon-Hotep (the peaceful Amon), was brought up in this zooletic catechism of the ram, while his young wife arrived from Heliopolis... where she had just left the House-of-Life of the priests of Aten! And this explains why, since she who was Queen Tyi had three daughters and a son: the one who became Amenophis IV before becoming the divine mortal Akhen-Aton!

But let's not get ahead of ourselves, because from the age of thirteen, one solar revolution after his coronation, the young pharaoh set off on faraway hunts organised for him by the priests of Amun. For four years, they were his only passions. From his seventeenth year onwards, he became morose and fell under the domination of his wife. As she bore him only three daughters, a latent disunity, which continued to grow, did not help the affairs of this young "Elder". Torn apart by the priests of Amun and the constant quarrels with the queen, Amenhetep III set about building great and magnificent edifices. A gigantic temple was erected facing the desert, on the west bank of the Nile, not far from Thebes. Not a single stone remains, except for the two monumental statues in his likeness, each nineteen metres high, that guarded the main façade. Posterity has named them the "Colossi of Memnon".

The interior of Luxor Temple also dates from this reign, bearing the imprint of the wealth of the time. His residence was a light but very luxuriously decorated building. To enhance the desert panorama, Queen Tyi had an immense lake dug, connected by a canal to the river, and around which she had thousands of fragrant trees planted. It was here that she gave birth to her three daughters. But constant quarrelling separated the couple for a long time. They did not reconcile until sixteen years later, when Queen Tyi finally gave birth to a son who was given the name of Amon-Hotep IV.

In the meantime, the king, unable to do without wives, sent for foreign princesses to be his concubines. It is likely that he was expecting one or more sons from them, but they never came. Or rather, if there was indeed a son, Queen Tyi made him disappear on the very day of his birth and replaced him in the mother's bed with a daughter!

The royal wife, although small and corpulent, had eyes that reflected a superior intelligence. She knew what she wanted and certainly didn't hesitate to use whatever means necessary to achieve it.

If the Mitanian princess Gilu-Hepa, who arrived in Thebes with an escort of three hundred ladies-in-waiting, had only two daughters before sinking into madness, relegated to the harem, the same could not be said of a certain Babylonian princess who gave birth at the hands of Queen Tyi herself, who took great care of her health. Need I add that this concubine only had a daughter to look at when she opened her eyes? In fact, she had been given a high dose of sleeping pills to prevent her suffering too much pain!

After all these "setbacks", a reconciliation between the two spouses took place. Queen Tyi left for Heliopolis to ask Aten for the grace of a divine male birth. The interesting thing to note here is that, from that day onwards, Aten was represented as dominating the Celestial Bull, which gave rise to the double-meaning name of:

AmonHapy, which in hieroglyphic as well as in Greek phonetisation became the equivalent of Amenophis. The destiny of the new-born, a boy, was already mapped out: he would be the ancient God-Unic reincarnated as the God of Aten. Finally, and most importantly, Queen Tyi had brought with her from Heliopolis one of the most prominent priests of her College: the Pontiff Taï. As soon as he saw that the newborn child was a boy, he obtained the king's permission and funds to build a temple to Aten within the walls of Thebes itself, among the other buildings dedicated to Amun!

To say that the priests were appalled would be an understatement! You have to understand that they were the undisputed masters of everything and everyone. Not only did they have exclusive rights to higher education, they also had the right to appoint scholars in all administrative and political disciplines.

Seeing themselves thus excluded from the official ceremonies could only inflame their hatred and desire for revenge. For the baptism of the future Pêr-Ahâ took place under the auspices of Aten, that is to say the double blessing of the Sun and the Celestial Bull, which had contained him for more than two millennia.

On the day foreseen by the particularly beneficial influences of the Twelve, a great mass was held to celebrate this baptism. There was no great crowd, as the people were still under the control of Amun, who distributed jobs and wealth exclusively to his followers. But the princes of the royal court, and above all the foreigners, who were very numerous in Thebes at the time, largely filled the temple aisles.

It was the Pontiff Taï himself who officiated, according to the traditional principles taught in Heliopolis for over a century and which had replaced those of Denderah buried under the sands and the wear and tear of time. There is no shortage of historical documents on this event, for let's not forget that we are now close to the famous biblical times of the Mosaic era. Not only is there no shortage of landmarks, but all the texts agree. This narrative is therefore easy to follow.

In this temple surrounded by a double row of superbly engraved colonnades, the walls were covered in electrum, the floor paved with silver, and the double doors covered with gold plates. The blue-azure ceiling was studded with five-pointed golden stars. Its opulence offered one of the most splendid spectacles imaginable, according to those who reported on the details of the ceremony at the time. In fact, the ceremony took on a solemn form long forgotten by the participants. For these priests of Aten, it was a return to the ancestral rites recommended by Ptah. And it was well before dawn that Taï gathered his priests to complete the perfect organisation of the historic baptism that would restore Aten's reputation while resurrecting Ptah.

A good hour before the Sun appeared on the horizon of Aten, the officiants designated as "Priests of the Birth of Aten", accompanied by the Scribe of the Rites and the Reader of the Solar Ritual, followed the "High Priest of the Pure Hands" in charge of preparing the Great Ceremony. Near the Sanctuary, they found the Pontiff, who had been praying all night in this holy place. An ascetic at heart, and instinctively aware that he was about to play the divine card almost double or nothing, various expiatory prayers had prepared him for the purification that was about to take place, purging him beforehand of any evil deeds that might be in his mind at the time.

Just as the officiants appeared, Tai arrived ahead of them, as if moved by a sixth sense. They continued on their way in silence, until they reached the gilded double doors of the eastern gate, set off even further by two large circular colonnades painted red.

Two priests pushed an already half-open door a little further, and it slid open without a sound, revealing the rising causeway that slid into the night over the wall surrounding the outbuildings to isolate them from the religious building itself, while providing direct access to the Sacred Lake.

For on this auspicious day of Celestial Combinations, the Pontiff also wanted to revive another tradition, which consisted of going to the Sacred Lake to purify himself directly, rather than merely undergoing a symbolic purification before any important ceremony.

Once this had been done, they all donned their tunics of unbleached linen, specially prepared for this exclusive use by the weaver-priests, who had been waiting there for a long time, attentive to the slightest defect likely to hinder their movements. The long, smouldering torches gave the scene a ritualistic quality that satisfied Taï's soul.

As if in a perfectly timed ballet, the four officiating priests silently made their way to the well of the Most Pure Spring, to bring back the jugs filled and purified the previous day, each containing eight litres of this water, which they were to transfer into a reservoir in the shape of a small bathtub, consecrated and kept away from any impure touching in the sacristy, in anticipation of the ceremony.

This room, adjoining the centre of the choir, was forbidden to anyone who had not purified themselves before entering.

In this way, the little bathtub would not reach its destination until the baby had to be immersed in it. All defilement was therefore diverted away from this place where the Water of Life would perform its complementary divine function in order to bring the new, still fragile soul into line with its future destiny, which would link it closely to its father: Aten.

The preliminary operations were so well organised that an uninitiated onlooker would have thought they had been going on for centuries without interruption!

The sky was just beginning to lighten in a rapid but measured progression when the preparations were completed. The priests opened wide the two doors of the main façade, so that guests and onlookers could experience the moment when a Son would receive his name as Man.

The violet of the Aten horizon flushed, turning bright red and orange. Any moment now, the gold of the first rays of the Sun would appear in the great aisle of the temple.

In somewhat stealthy shadows, the guests hurried in, spreading out in the bays close to the christening altar. Suddenly, the gold of the sky filled the building, haloing it in dazzling hues through all the openings in the top of the east wall. And as if waiting only for this celestial manifestation, the Pêr-Ahâ appeared, carried by eight priests, on his chair inlaid with gold and jewels. Then Queen Tyi, the "Goddess of the Two Lands", entered in her turn, arousing a general murmur of admiration. She held her son close to her, having left it to no-one else to present him for baptism.

Taï approached her without worrying too much about what the king would do. He took the baby gently and stroked its cheeks, while Tyi descended alone from her portable throne. Amenhotep III took longer to extricate himself from his throne, as all his traditional ornaments were cumbersome and quite heavy. In addition, his illness was developing rapidly and he was beginning to suffer horribly, although he tried not to show it too much. And the king thought it was time to make peace not only with his wife on this occasion, but also with those priests of a different denomination from the one in which he had been brought up, but who had given him this son in his own image.

Meanwhile, the Pontiff had approached the holy table and all the guests were seated. Taï raised the baby above him, towards the rays of the rising sun, saying in a loud voice:

- O you, who rise day after day on the horizon willed by Aten; O you, Ra, who sail with regularity over the Earth to fertilise it season after season, you are the blessing of Aten, the Almighty Creator. You appear radiant with divine light as soon as you appear on the horizon of Aten. You follow the invisible celestial river that he traces out for you, sailing eternally in your sacred boat, never changing course.

The choir of priests hastened to repeat the last sentence in the form of a litany:

- You sail eternally, O Ra, in your sacred boat, never changing course!

At this point, the four officiants hurried to light their censers at a waiting brandon. They each went around the altar to complete the purification. Then they went to fetch the little bathtub, while Taï returned the baby to its mother for a moment to go to the pedestal of the Prophet and intone a prayer of intercession to Aten:

- O You, who come from Hapy, the Celestial Bull, in your manifestation of Aten, grant to this ceremony of the baptism of your Son all your beneficial influences so that his name of Man may be the sign of the faithful servant he will be to you and to his people.

The priest reading the new ritual, who had approached the Pontiff, took over, raising both arms above his head in supplication:

- O You, who are the offspring of Hapy, the Celestial Bull, grant that this newborn child here present may serve You, Aten, who fashioned the Great Luminary which, each morning, generates by its radiance, each beneficial day on this earth. We pray you with renewed fervour that it may be so, day after day, from this moment when this little being will receive his name of Man, and that he may make good use of it during his very long earthly life.

The Pontiff Taï, who had sunk into deep meditation during this imploration, reopened his eyelids and stared at the guests, before intoning in a firm voice the ritual he had devised:

- Glory to the father of us all: Aton.

The phrase was taken up in chorus by those present, as were all the others that followed. After a few hesitations, the long litany to this new God, yet at the same time so ancient, enthused all those present. If there was a spy sent by the priests of Amon, he would have an edifying report to make! The end in particular was enough to make them shudder from the pedestal on which they had placed themselves, for Taï had ended with this conclusion that one of his colleagues in Denderah would not have disowned:

- Eternity is Yours, O Aten! The origin of all our lives comes from your radiance on all beings wherever they may be, your beneficial protection extending everywhere under our sky. There is no protection more powerful than yours, which granted this little being to take on his human form and give him his name of Man.

Tai paused briefly, raising an accusing index finger to the crowd of guests:

- Anyone who enters this holy place with impure thoughts will suffer the repercussions even in the Beyond of this earthly life. Aton is peaceful in his creation, which does not tolerate disagreement or slaughter. But he himself will severely punish those who break his heavenly Commandments. Purity is the most beautiful adornment that Aten has bestowed on our souls. It is Purity above all that I pray with all my strength to penetrate the Divine Parcel already in this infant body, and to inspire it with the goodness and righteousness that will be eternally in it.

The officiants, who returned just then, carrying the bath, were preceded by two priests who unfolded rolls of fine cloth woven in gold on the altar, on which the baptismal basin was placed. During this time, harpists sang a song of praise in honour of the couple, drawing melodious sounds from their instruments.

With everything finally ready, Taï approached the altar:

- May Aton bless this taking possession of His human quality from a fleshly envelope that has just been born, for He is here in His earthly Abode. It is in the arms of His submissive daughter, the goddess of the Two Lands, that He finds Himself, and whom His grace must fill with its benefits.

There was a murmur in the audience, for it was becoming clear that the next Pêr-Ahâ, the one who was silently waving his little hands, would be the son of Aten, and not of Amun, like his father who was there unperturbed in his royal finery, and like his ancestral predecessors had been.

The priest of the Ritual, always present next to the Pontiff, made an imperative sign to the congregation to rise while he articulated in a slow but strong voice:

- That the Pêr-Ahâ "Hapy", from the Land of Ath

Let Kâ-Ptah come forward to this table; let the divine Tyi approach us to present her son to Aten!

The two spouses came before the altar, Amun-Hapy having pretended not to notice the censoring of his title of Amun in his name by the priest of the Ritual. The queen took off the beautiful tunic covering her child's body and presented him to the Pontiff.

Holding it carefully, Tai raised it above the bath and said:

- Blessed is the one who lives in justice and goodness, for he will be able to contemplate your face without being blinded by it, O Aten! Since you are the god of all generosity, may this baby boy, your venerated Son, grow up in obedience to your commandments. Let us first raise our voices in common prayer for the fulfilment of this wish.

Strangely enough, all the throats then uttered, without any concertation, the ancient prayer of Ptah, learnt long before, and practically forgotten to this day. Then, lowering the body slowly into the bath, the Pontiff continued:

- In this Living Water, coming from the sacred source that you have been irradiating for millions of years, O Aton, make your Wisdom, your Purity and your Justice, together with the Great Ra of the Great Celestial River, the vital principles of this little body, your Son for ever, as soon as it has been immersed the traditional three times in this baptismal liquid that has been specially consecrated to you.

The first immersion was gentle. The whole body disappeared into the bath full of pure water. Taï supported the little head, however, an instinctive movement of recoil having arched this still very delicate camel envelope. The Pontiff smiled inwardly at this, before continuing, bringing the dripping baby above his head:

- The second immersion in this Water full of the Living Forces of Aten, so that this Parcel of yourself which is its soul pursues a path parallel to that which is yours between our two horizons. May it retain its most brilliant brilliance, of unblemished fairness, and of a fullness equal to that of the Eternal Sun.

And Taï plunged the baby back into the bath. This time, the arms flailed and the mouth let out a resounding "aâ-rê" in understandable protest. But the future great king did not cry. And the Pontiff, speeding up the proceedings of the ceremony, quickly raised the body to his eye level, before continuing:

- Finally, this third immersion of Water, radiant with your eternal glory, so that this now immortal soul follows not only the same path as yours, but your Commandments that will enable our Second Heart to survive into the Eternity that is yours, and which is perfectly defined by the rhythmic cycles of your great years.

This time, the baby didn't cry out when it came into contact with the water. He even smiled as he reappeared from the wave, the sun's rays suddenly hitting his face. Taï, for his part, gave a joyous, but internal, laugh of satisfaction, the Sun being well on schedule according to the calculations of his masters of Numbers! But as two of the officers approached the queen with thick cloths to wrap around her quivering body, he put on his solemn face and handed the son to his mother.

After wiping him tenderly, Tyi passed him his beautiful tunic and handed him back to the venerable Patriarch. All this time, the king had retained the rigidity of a statue. Having agreed to finance the construction of this religious edifice to a god other than Amun in gratitude for having given him a son, he could say nothing. In fact, he didn't even want to. He had grown old, and now he had to think about securing the place that should be his in the afterlife.

During this time of profound silence, Taï had raised the body as high as possible above his head so that all the guests could see it clearly. This is how he ended this memorable ceremony:

- O You, Lord of eternal life in your Aten form, here is this child of a man and a woman. From this day on, you alone will control his destiny. Make it as brilliant and noble as yours. Welcome at this moment into your register of great souls the one whose name will henceforth be synonymous with Divine Mortal for our future Annals: "The Mirror of Aten", for it will be your exact reflection for all Eternity." Eternal life to the Divine Mortal Akh-en-Aton!"

The priests and officiants repeated this last sentence with an emphasis that echoed in the ears of everyone present:

"Eternal life to the divine mortal Akh-en-Aton!"

The ceremony for the baptism of the man who was to shake the idolatrous power of Amun the godless to its foundations was over. The guests scattered across the temple's vast esplanade, looking contrite and dismayed before the mocking gazes of the common people who had come to witness from afar the exit of those whom their priests were beginning to openly describe as renegades.

The golden chariots were waiting for their occupants and the magnificent horses pulling them were chomping at the bit. But it was necessary to wait for the royal couple to emerge before leaving the precincts of the temple. They soon appeared, seated on their gilded portable thrones, resting on the shoulders of palace servants, while bearers of long-sleeved ostrich feather fans ran to the sides, waving them so that the flies, which were plentiful at this time of year, would not bother the faces of the august figures whose engraving would last forever.

The baby, the divine mortal, slept peacefully in his mother's arms, still unaware of the torrent of passions he was about to unleash in Thebes! But as this unique and extraordinary life will be the subject of the next volume, let's leave him to pursue his childish dreams without disturbing him any further.

On the other hand, his father, whom no one dared to call by his divine name, Amun-Hopet, but by that of Amun-Hapy, more in keeping with the celestial views of Aten, was increasingly affected in the serenity of his soul. During these terrible years, the religious struggles for influence intensified, increasingly disrupting life in the opulent Theban capital.

The historical documents handed down to us from the annals of that time indicate that the king, who was entering the thirtieth year of his reign, had a mortuary chapel built next to his tomb in the valley beyond the earthly life, where all his predecessors were buried.

But this pharaoh, who had incurred the hatred of both clergies, was very much afraid that his sarcophagus would be violated once it had been deposited in his underground dwelling. So he appealed "to the gods" to ensure that a terrible punishment, and the curse of the Lord, would not befall those who tried to damage anything on the burial site that would be his.

This was his last "sensible" act, and he died six years later, in 1370 BC. A few months before his death, however, an event occurred that should be recounted to close this third volume of the history of monotheism, because it is indicative of the latent antagonism that separated the two enemy clans of the same family for millennia and millennia.

So, for once, the priests of Amun and Aten wished Amenhotep dead, as he no longer appeared in public. Everyone claimed that this was the heavenly punishment for the man who had aroused the divine anger. And the king, in a last flash of lucidity, sent a message to one of his 'fathers-in-law', whose daughter was a Mitanian princess, to send him the miraculous statue of Ishtar that he had in his palace in Nineveh! This was obviously the worst affront for those of Amun, since his reminiscence with Isis could not upset those of Aten too much.

It's easy to imagine the looks on the faces of the priests and the city's one million inhabitants, crowded in close ranks from the eastern gate to the royal palace to watch the surprising procession pass by!

A hundred or so priests with curly beards, high hairstyles that were surprising for those who usually only saw shaven heads, and their bodies and clothes hidden by very thick dark woollen cloaks - it was enough to render an uninformed public speechless with astonishment!

Twenty-four priests, no less, were needed to carry the divine Ishtar. And the sight of these clerics sweating from every visible pore of their skin was not the least surprising aspect of the scene. Others were playing strange, shrill instruments, while still others were banging away on huge drums.

But Ishtar was not the healer they had hoped for, and the priests of the King of Mitanni returned to the north of their native Syria more quietly than they had arrived!

And the "Goddess of the Two Lands", the divine Tyi, ruled the country with the help of the Pontiff Tai, waiting for her son, the divine mortal Akhen-Aton, to come of age and take the reins of power in his own hands, under the enlightened guidance of Aten.

CHAPTER XIII

THE DYNASTIC CHRONOLOGY OF ATH-KA-PTAH

> *"Nevertheless, we must admit that the conclusions reached by the Egyptologists who enjoy great authority in France and Germany - Lepsius, Bunsen, Brugsch and Boëck - are not entirely in line with the figures for the years recorded in the Bible from Adam to Abraham.*
>
> BISHOP MEIGNAN,
> BISHOP OF CHALONS.
> *(The World and Primitive Man, 1869).*

The starting point for this chronology, which is commonly accepted, was the unification of the country by Mena, or Menes, during a Sirius-Sun conjunction, as stated in the texts, which occurred only once every 1,461 years.

And it is from this starting point that the stories differ. Those in favour of a long chronology, such as Champollion, start from 5867 BC; those in favour of a short chronology, such as M. de Bunsen and Weigrul, start nearly three millennia later. Between these two clans, there is the multitude of seasoned Egyptologists who are not concerned with astronomical judgements, but with historical suppositions such as the possibility of two concurrent reigns in Upper and Lower Egypt to reduce or increase the time allotted to one of the first thirty dynasties.

As a preamble, and before going into more detail about the mathematical value of the revolution of the Sep'ti "Fix", or Sothis in Greek, and Sirius in French, in the calculations of the duration of the Pharaonic reigns since Menes, let us note below the year 1 found by the distinguished researchers of the 19th century, to leave those of our own time with their own incomprehensions:

Champollion	5867 BC
Lesieur	5773 BC
Boeck	5702 BC
Hensy	5303 BC
Lenormant	5124 BC
Mariette	5004 BC
de Saulcy	4717 BC
Brugsh	4455 BC
Lepsius	3892 BC
of Bunsen	3623 BC
Weigall	3407 BC

This is obviously only a small sample of the authors who worked on the Egyptian annals before compiling a chronological account. There are still two chronological schools of thought among modern Egyptologists: the short and the long.

Let's look at it logically, with astronomical and mathematical precision, to see exactly what the situation is, because rigour is absolutely essential here.

The star Sirius was used as a fixed point in the original calendar, and there is no doubt about that, as thousands of pieces of evidence attest. This absolute calculation was carried out by the first masters of Measurement and Number. To make things easier to understand, we'll keep the Greek name of this star, Sothis, because in astronomy, it's always referred to as "the Sothian period of 1,461 years", which is the celestial rotation time of this star in our sky.

A little fact that I noted in one of the previous chapters of this volume is that in Denderah, for example, every year Sothis rises for the first time, above the horizon, six hours later than the previous year. This means that every four years this star will be a day late. Now, since there are 1,460 solar days (365 1/4× 4) and we have to add one for leap year, that makes 1,461 days per solar cycle. The same applies to Sirius, which was used as the mathematical basis for the calculations, but over 1,461 years instead of 1,461 days. And at the end of this Year of God, the Sothian cycle ended with a very precise conjunction of the Sun and Sirius at their similar sunrises. There was no arithmetical shift in either space or time in the harmonic movements, whereas even today, despite the addition of a leap day, there is still a gap in time that can only be made up in several centuries, which is a great pity.

How can we re-establish the ancient dating of the chronology in such conditions? We have several points of reference. The most commonly accepted, and very valid, one is provided by the Latin historian Censorinus. In his XXIth chapter, he notes that just a century before he wrote his text, the first day of Thoth in the Egyptian calendar fell "on the extraordinary day of the rising of the heatwave in Egypt", the equivalent of our 19th of July in the year 139 AD.

Another major contribution to chronological compilation was the discovery, in 1865, of the text of the "Decree of Canopus". The preface states that in year 9 of the reign of Ptolemy III Euergetes[62], the rising of Sothis took place on the 1st of Payni, the first day of the 10th month of the year.

The Decree was as follows:

"In order that the months follow an absolute rule, in accordance with the natural order of the world, and that it no longer happens that certain solemn feasts celebrated in winter are celebrated in summer, the progress of the star advancing by one day every four years, and that other feasts among those which are now celebrated in summer are celebrated later in winter as has already happened before, and would still happen if the year remained composed of 360 days and 5 days instituted under the name of epagomena, from now on, one day will be added... "

---

[62] So in the year 238 BC, or 377 years before Censorinus. That's just over a quarter of the Sothian revolution, which makes it possible to estimate very precisely the length of the heatwave year. The Dog, or Canicule in Latin, is the symbol of Sirius.

A concrete example of the chronological value of this astronomical source is the dating of the beginning of the reign of Amenophis I, of the XVIIIth dynasty, who was the founder of the family of which Akhenaten was the fourth reigning Pharaoh.

Another papyrus, this one discovered by the German Egyptologist G. Ebers, reads: "In Year 9 of the reign of His Majesty Amonhotep, Health and Eternal Life to him who has the Right Voice, and more precisely on the Day of the Year of the rising of Sep'ti, the 9th day of the 3rd month of Shemou, the King..".

The calculation of the precise date is crucial here, because it provides mathematically and without any possible controversy the date of the beginning of the reign of Amenhetep I[er], and hence the very beginning of the XVIIIth Dynasty, since this only had the famous Yahmes, or Amosis as predecessor to Amenhetep.

The delay between the 1st day of Thoth in the year 139 of Censorinus and the 9th day of the 3rd month of Shemou, which is the 11th month of the year, is 56 days. Now, as there has been an extra complete "heatwave" cycle, there has been an additional shift of 365 days by a quarter for the 1,461 years. This gives: $56 + 365\ 1/4 = 421$ days $1/4$, or a time lapse of 1,685 years, obtained by multiplying by four for the shift of one day every four years of Sothis in Space.

Starting from the year 139 AD and going back 1,685 years, we obtain the date 1546 BC, the ninth year of the reign of Amenophis I[er]. So the Pharaoh was crowned in the year 1555, an irrefutable mathematical date.

Given that, here too, all the aforementioned Egyptologists give different dates, it's food for thought! After all, even for those unfamiliar with the Ebers papyrus, the astronomical key was provided by the two "classics" known the world over: the Canopic Decree and Censorin's dating.

The calculation is very simple:

The Decree announces the first day of the rising of Sirius for the 1st Payni of the year 238 BC, and Censorin for the 1st of Thot of the year 139 AD, i.e. in 377 years, a difference of:
29 days for the month of Payni,
30 days for Epiphi,
30 days for Mésori,
5 epagomenal days to return to the 1st of Thot
i.e. a gap of 94 days.

Now, 94 days' difference, at the rate of one every 4 years, gives (94× 4) the 376 years separating 238 before from the start of 139 after.

Similarly, it is easy to calculate the start of the chronology, as Athothis re-established the hieroglyphic system on the day of the conjunction of the Sun and Sirius, after a two-year reign.

Starting from the 1st day of Thoth 139, backwards, by 3× 1 461 years, we get 4 382 years. We need to subtract 139 for the date to start before Christ, i.e. the 1st day of Thoth 4244. His reign therefore began two years earlier with the death of the Unifier Menes, in 4246 BC.

Here, then, is the "Chronology of Ath-Ka-Ptah", up to Amenopis III of the XVIIIth Dynasty, as proclaimed by the "natural order of the world" of the famous Decree of Canopus.

ALPHABETICAL INDEX OF HIEROGLYPHIC WORDS

HIEROGLYPHIC names	Names GREEKS	Duration Kingdom	Dating (BC)	RENEWAL highlight
1ère DYNASTIE				
	MENES	62	4308-4246	Was the unifier of the fratricidal Deux-Clans.
	ATHOTHIS	55	4248-4191	Restorer of Hieroglyphics
	ATHOTHIS II	31	4195-4160[63]	
	HENEPHTYS	19	4160-4141	She was the first Queen. She had to fight a very serious famine
	OUANEPHES	23	4141-4118	
	OUSIRPHERES	20	4118-4098	
	MIEVIS	26	4098-4072	Left his capital, Thinis, to go to the Delta
	SEMEMPSIS	18	4073-4054	A violent plague killed 1/3 of the people.
	BINOCHIS	26	4054-4028	

There were therefore eight kings and one queen during this first dynasty. Manetho has "omitted" to mention the name and time of Henephthys, which makes 280 years of reign.

With the next sceptre-bearers, the difference is very clear, as the worshippers of the Sun appear, opposed by those of the Bull "Hapy", introduced at Men-Fer, the Memphis of the Greeks, and Ath-Kâ-Ptah.

---

[63] The differences in dates between the end of one reign and the beginning of another stem from years of co-regency with the previous Pharaoh.

Hieroglyphic names	Names GREEKS	Duration Kingdom	Dating (BC)	RENEWAL highlight
IIe DYNASTY				
	BENRES	38	4028-3990	Its name means: "The Sun attracts it".
	KATEKHOS	39	3990-3951	Re-establishes the cult of the Hapy Bull.
	BINOTHRIS	47	3955-3906	Reinstituted matriarchal law.
	TELAS	17	3906-3889	
	SETHENES	41	3889-3848	First king Ahâ of Set.
	CHERES	17	3848-3831	Adds the solar title of Ra, or Ra to his name.
	NEFERCHERES	25	3831-3806	Meaning: "There were two of them".
	SESOCHRES	48	3808-3758	
	CHENERES	30	3758-3728	Restores the union by marrying a defeated princess from the North.

There were therefore nine kings in this second dynasty, which lasted three hundred and two years. From the nineteenth king onwards, he bore all the titles of the unified Two-Clans: the Ahâ is: King Sparrowhawk and Set, King Reed and Bee, Lord Cobra and Vulture. All surmounted by the Sun.

IIIe DYNASTY				
	NECHEROPHES	28	3728-3700	The Pacific. Having subdued the South, he reigns in peace.

Hieroglyphic names	Names GREEKS	Duration Kingdom	Dating (BC)	RENEWAL highlight
	DJEZER	29	3702-3671	Builder of the Step Pyramid in Sakarâ.
	TYRES	7	3671-3664	
	MESOCHRES	17	3664-3647	
	SOUPHIS	16	3647-3631	
	OUSIRTASIS	19	3631-3612	
	ACHES	42	3612-3570	
	KERPHERES	26	3570-3544	
	SNEFROU	31	3544-3513	With this reign, painting and sculpture were at the zenith of their art.

There were nine kings in this third dynasty, which lasted two hundred and fifteen years. With this Pêr-Ahâ, equality between all men was not an illusion, as all the drawings attest, for there are no scenes of savagery anywhere at this time.

IVth DYNASTY

	KHORIS	29	3513-3484	
	KHEOPS	63	3484-3421	It was this king who usurped numerous monuments. Built the 2(th) pyramid.
	KHEFREN	66	3421-3355	

Hieroglyphic names	Names GREEKS	Duration Kingdom	Dating (BC)	RENEWAL highlight
	MYKHERINOS	62	3355-3293	Built the 3rd pyramid.
	TAISERES	25	3293-3268	
	BICHERES	22	3268-3246	
	SEBERCHERES	7	3246-3239	
	THAMPHTYS	9	3239-3230	

There were eight kings in this fourth dynasty, which lasted two hundred and eighty-three years. Money troubles got the better of the last Ahâ, who gave way to a line of nobles arriving from Elephantine to take power.

Ve DYNASTIE

Hieroglyphic	Name	Duration	Dating	Renewal
	OUSIRCHERES	28	3230-3208	This is where the use of the title "Son of Geb" comes in: "Son of Geb".
	SEPHRES	13	3208-3195	
	NEFERCHERES II	20	3195-3175	
	NOUSIRES	7	3175-3168	
	SCHOUHOR	20	3168-3148	Tried to take back the Sceptre for Horus.
	RATHOURES	44	3148-3104	

HIEROGLYPHIC names	Names GREEKS	Duration Kingdom	Dating (BC)	RENEWAL highlight
	MENCHERES	9	3104-3095	
	DJEKARES	43	3095-3052	Took the title of: "Son of the Sun".
	OUNAS	34	3052-3018	His cartouche was found as far as Byblos.

There were nine kings during this Vth dynasty of two hundred and eighteen years. The Elephantine kings ceased to hold the throne, only to cede it again to the Memphis kings. After the reign of Uanas, the close relationship between the clergy of Re and the Memphite court was abandoned.

VIe DYNASTIE

	TEPHTAH	8	3018-3010	His funeral mask was made shortly after his murder.
	CHOUSIRES	22	3010-2988	
	MERIRA-PEPI	53	2988-2935	
	MERENRES	4	2935-2931	This "pharaoh" held the sceptre at the age of seven, and died at eleven!
	MENTOUH OTEPH	14	2931-2917	
	PEPI II	97	2917-2820	An interminable reign that led to total anarchy.
	MENESOUPHIS	1	2820-2819	Was murdered.

After these seven kings, the VIth dynasty came to an end. And for six years, the country fell prey to decadence. Temples were ruined, tombs violated and looted. The collapse was total after 1,500 years of splendour and power. The exact time for one revolution of the star Sirius: 1,461 years. Then came Neterkaré, who founded the next dynasty, whose sister is recorded in the annals.

Hieroglyphic names	Names GREEKS	Duration Kingdom	Dating (BC)	RENEWAL highlight
VIIe DYNASTY				
	NETERCHARES	3	2813-2810	Was murdered.
	NITOCHRIS	12	2810-2798	Avenged his brother by poisoning the killers at a famous banquet.

He was succeeded by three other kings, whose short reigns have left us with no names, all their cartridges having been hammered! The VIIIth Dynasty is no more prolific, despite the nineteen kings who held the reins of Egypt for one hundred and twenty-three years. What is certain is that each province governed itself as it saw fit, according to the vices of the ruler! This happy people, so proud of their virtues, had just fallen into the worst kind of torpor.

IXe DYNASTIE

There were four successive Khêti kings: Ouakharê, Meribrê, Nebkaourê and Mérikarê. They reigned for fifty-three years, mainly in the north, with Hierakleopolis as their capital. The total length of this dynasty is one hundred and eighty-two years. The Xth dynasty, which rebelled in the south and reigned simultaneously, but in continuous struggles, lasted one hundred and sixteen years, and it is impossible to mention the names of the one hundred and nineteen "kings", or those who claimed to be such!

XIe DYNASTIE

	MENTOUHOTEP 1	8	2426-2418	He founded the dynasty of which Thebes was the capital.
	MENTOUHOTEP 2	9	2418-2409	
	MENTOUHOTEP 3	46	2409-2363	

Names HIEROGLYPHIC	Names GREEKS	Duration Kingdom	Dating (BC)	RENEWAL highlight
105	MENTOUHOTEP 4	18	2363-2345	A terrible famine marked the decline of the dynasty.
106	MENTOUHOTEP 5	7	2345-2338	Died prematurely.
107	MENTOUHOTEP 6	4	2338-2334	Was dethroned.

There were six kings during this ninety-second dynasty. The new pharaoh, who was chosen from among the rulers, benefited from a very abundant flooding of the Nile, which led to superb harvests and an end to famine. The first Theban period continued, with the king covering with gold the cult and temples of Amun that were taking off.

XIIe DYNASTIE

Hieroglyphic	Name	Duration	Dating	Renewal
	AMONHEMES I	32	2334-2302	Chased off the Hycksos who were beginning to infiltrate
	SESOSTRIS I	42	2302-2260	
	AMONHEMES II	29	2260-2231	
	SESOSTRIS II	19	2231-2212	
	SESOSTRIS III	45	2212-2167	He was the greatest, and Herodotus praised his battles.
	AMONHEMES III	49	2167-2128	Carrying out major clean-up work.
	AMONHEMES IV	3	2118-2115	Died suddenly. With no male heir, the sceptre went to a princess who

					died shortly afterwards.
		SEBECHERET	4	2115-2111	

Thus ended this XIIth dynasty, which, with seven kings and one queen, lasted two hundred and twenty-three years. The wealth and omnipotence of the Theban clergy caused the kingship to crumble once again, leaving the new dynasty without a solid foundation.

Names HIEROGLYPHIC	Names GREEKS	Duration Kingdom	Dating (BC)	RENEWAL highlight
XIIIe DYNASTIE				
116	CHOUTARES	5	2111-2106	Died suddenly
117	CHEMCHOURES	2	2106-2104	His untimely death led to further unrest.

In the sixty-one years that followed, twenty-one kings and two queens succeeded each other, but in fact they only reigned for a total of sixty-two years, as several of them reigned jointly in Upper and Lower Egypt! The Hycksos were already establishing themselves in the north, and their tribes of shepherds were fomenting the first disturbances.

The fourteenth and fifteenth dynasties were even more confused, with each province declaring itself autonomous and having its own "king"! Long and exhausting struggles lasted until one of the Semitic invaders, King Khian the Jonias of Manetho, had himself proclaimed pharaoh. He behaved like a true sceptre-bearer. His son, raised as a true prince of Egypt, brought peace and prosperity. But it was during these two reigns that the Jews settled on the banks of the Nile, including Joseph in year 17 of the reign of Apophis the First.

XVIe DYNASTIE				
	HAPENRES	26	1909-1883	

127	MACHIBRES	31	1883-1852	
(hieroglyph)	DOUDOUMES	23	1852-1829	
(hieroglyph)	DOUDOUMES II	46	1829-1783	

Names HIEROGLYPHIC	Names GREEKS	Duration Kingdom	Dating (BC)	RENEWAL highlight
(hieroglyph)	APOPHIS I	33	1783-1750	Arrival of Joseph in year 17 of the reign.
(hieroglyph)	CHEBEKEMSEPH	3	1750-1747	

Thus ended the 16th dynasty, with the decline of the Hycksos invaders. But this debacle led to new fratricidal struggles between the two indigenous clans of the descendants of Horus and Set. Manetho grants them an intermediate dynasty of thirty-nine kings who reigned for only one hundred and sixty-seven years, the XVIIth, which will not be enumerated for this reason.

XVIII[e] DYNASTIE

(hieroglyph)	AMOSIS	25	1580-1555	
(hieroglyph)	AMENOPHIS I	23	1558-1532	Was co-regent for three years.
(hieroglyph)	THOUTMOSIS I	12	1523-1520	
(hieroglyph)	THOUTMOSIS II	20	1522-1500	See very important note on next page.
(hieroglyph)	HATSCHEPSOUT	23	1500-1477	This is the Amenset of Manetho and Champollion.
(hieroglyph)	THOUTMOSIS III	30	1477-1447	
(hieroglyph)	AMENOPHIS II	35	1447-1412	

	THOUTMOSIS IV	9	1412-1403	
	AMENOPHIS III	36	1403-1367	
	AMENOPHIS IV	16	1367-1351	Changed his name to Akhenaten.

This dynasty was one of the longest and most brilliant in Egypt, due to the upheavals it brought about. It did not end with Amenophis IV - Akhenaten, but as this book stops at the birth of Akhenaten, the chronology will continue when subsequent volumes are published.

NOTE ON THE YEAR 1500 BC

(Moses and his people crossing the Red Sea)

As can be seen at the end of the preceding chronological table, Pharaoh Thutmes II died suddenly after a reign of twenty years. The Annals are silent on the cause of his death.

In the pages preceding the chronology, we explained and demonstrated that the reign Amenhetep Ibegan in 1555, that of Thutmes Iin 1532 and that the twenty-year reign of Thutmes II lasted from 1520 to 1500.

Now, this date of 1500 BC is very important on another level, which I have studied in detail elsewhere, and which the reader will be able to follow in full in the next volume to be published.

Precise dating is easier than it might seem at first sight, thanks to astronomical landmarks. All the errors made on this subject to this day stem from an attempt to interpret Manetho's texts. According to this Sybarite priest, it was under a king of the XVIIIth Dynasty that the Insurrection took place. Not just the Jews, of course, but all the fellahs too, oppressed by the usurpers. Now, it was Amosis who drove the Hycksos out of the country, and it was a Thutmose who pursued Moses.

But the ancient Greek authors who compiled them made several mistakes in these texts, as in so many other papyri! They transcribed Amenophis instead of Amosis, and, reading from left to right instead of the other way round, they placed Amenophis as the liberator of Moses, and Thutmosis as the pursuer of the Hycksos!...

As a result, Theophilus and the African, evaluating a chronology by Manetho according to the enumeration transcribed by Flavius Josephus, got bogged down in calculations proving that, since this was impossible (see the chronology), it was rather Seti and Ramses of the XIXth dynasty! This obviously distorted the biblical data compiled by the Fathers of the Church, who were forced to restrict the antiquity of times even further!

What do we know about the astronomical calendar? Clement of Alexandria, who had all the original elements preserved in the Library of Alexandria of which he was the Curator, assured us that the Exodus of the Jews occurred two centuries after the renewal of the canicular year subtracted from 22. This is crystal clear to anyone who has studied the revolutions of the stars. That of Sirius, the Greek Sothis, and *the Year of the Dog* for the ancient Egyptians, who thus imagined Anubis, the Guardian of Pure Souls. For in hieroglyphics, Sirius *is the Year of God.* The Dog is Latin for "heatwave", so this is the celestial revolution of this star. Since Sirius moves in 1,461 years, and began in 139 AD, it ended in 1322 BC. If we subtract the 178 years that elapsed after its renewal, the result is 1500, to be precise... the year of the death of Thutmose II, although the Annals do not say how or why. Why this deliberate obscurity, it seems?

Let's go back to the reign of Thutmose 1[er], the father of the man we are interested in. He had three sons and one daughter. As the two eldest sons died young, he focused all his affection on his daughter, the delightful Hatshepsut, seeming to completely ignore his youngest son. However, Thutmose I[er] was in delicate health and died in the twelfth year of his reign (in 1520, therefore), and it was naturally the younger son who was declared king under the name Djhathimes, or Thutmose II, to follow Manethonian phonetisation.

However, his mother was only a concubine of Thutmose 1st, whereas Princess Hathchepsut was the daughter of Hemtenphut, daughter of Amosis, and half-sister of the Pharaoh. Hathchepsut was therefore undoubtedly of much nobler blood... but she was still a delightful young girl of fifteen! And much to her chagrin, although the Queen Mother wanted to make her the bearer of the Sceptre, she was forced by the priests to marry her half-brother, Thutmose II, who was twenty years old, thus becoming, for better or for worse, only the Queen Consort.

Weak of character in front of his wife, embittered by playing only a secondary role, it is obvious that love did not reign over this couple. Nevertheless, two years later, a daughter, Nefrouret, was born. After that, the couple went their separate ways for quite a long time! And this Thutmose was gradually rejected by everyone in favour of his wife: a "strong head", whose constant demands against her husband's weakness bore fruit. And it was not long before she succeeded in her plot in the seventeenth year of Thutmes' reign, the date of his jubilee. But her husband, having been warned of the plot, and showing unusual strength, Hathchepsut made good her bad fortune and reconciled with her husband. This agreement led to the birth of a child, which was unfortunately another daughter! And misunderstandings returned to the household.

At this very moment, a son whom he had had with a concubine at the time of the first separation, reached his sixteenth birthday. He was doing his novitiate in the House-of-Life of the Priests of Amun when his father appointed him co-regent at his side as a sign of opprobrium against Hathchepsut. Righteous anger shook her, and it was probably this that prompted him, through the Council of Nobles in his pay, to pursue the Jews who were fleeing Egypt, but taking with them all the monotheistic Egyptians of Ptah-Un. They could no longer bear Amun's impious ascent to the azure "Heart" given by God to his creatures. It was therefore both a crime of lèse-majesté and the last hope of the queen consort to wish Pharaoh death. The death of the Pharaoh came suddenly during the chase, and nowhere did anyone mention how it happened - and with good reason!

Thutmes III then ascended the throne. In his biographical note, the royal architect writes: "Thutmose III became the Pêr-Ahâ on his father's throne. Queen consort Hathchepsut, however, governed Egypt because of her abilities.

It was therefore she who ordered that no mention should be made of the end of the previous Pharaoh. Hathchepsut's abilities were such that in the ninth year of the reign of Thutmes III, she finally succeeded in having herself proclaimed Pharaoh under the name of Maatkara.

To conclude this note, it is safe to say that it was in 1500 BC that Moses crossed the Red Sea with his people (Jews and Egyptians together under his halo as Prince of Egypt). They were pursued by the army of Thutmose II. It was during this campaign that the Pharaoh died suddenly. Was it a violent death during an assassination plotted by henchmen in the pay of Queen Hathchepsut? Or was it when he tried to pursue the Jews across the Red Sea? That's another story, to which you'll have to refer, dear reader, very soon!

OTHER TITLES

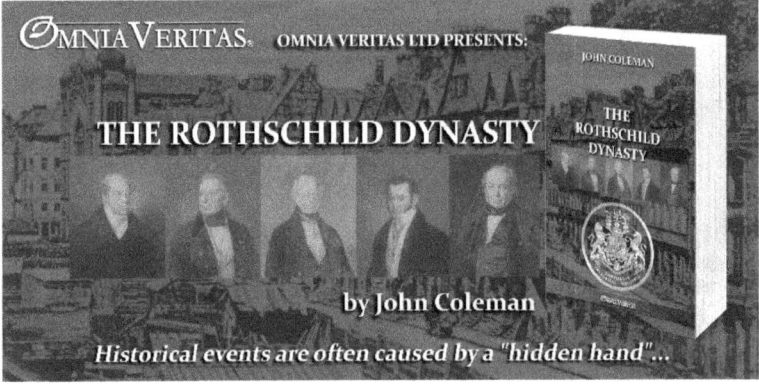

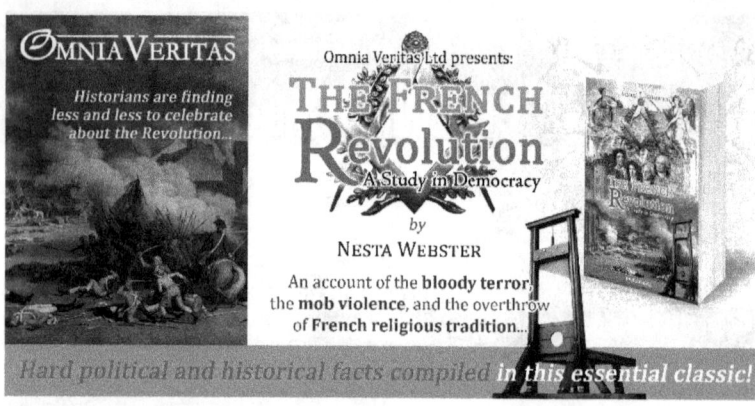

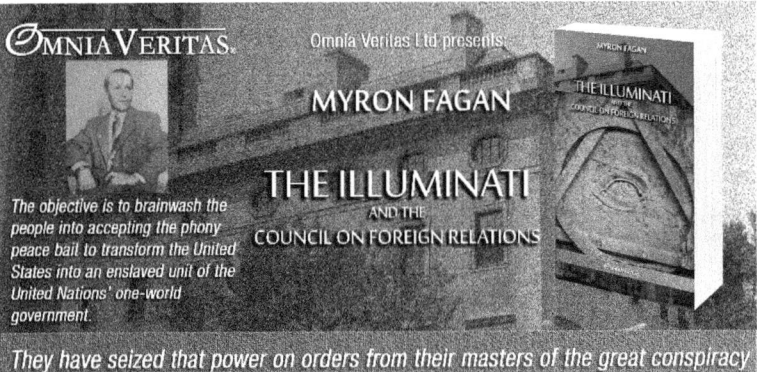

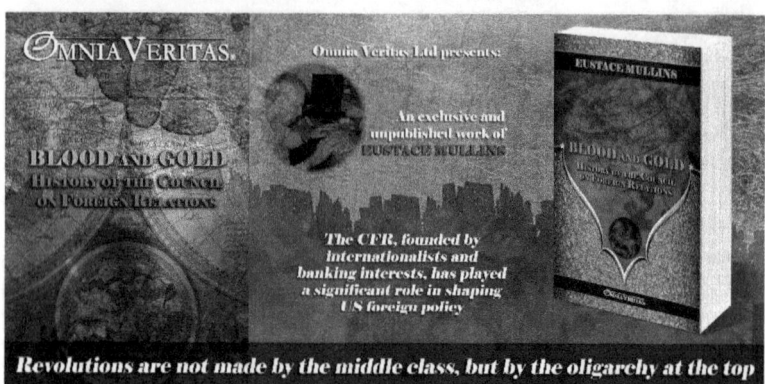

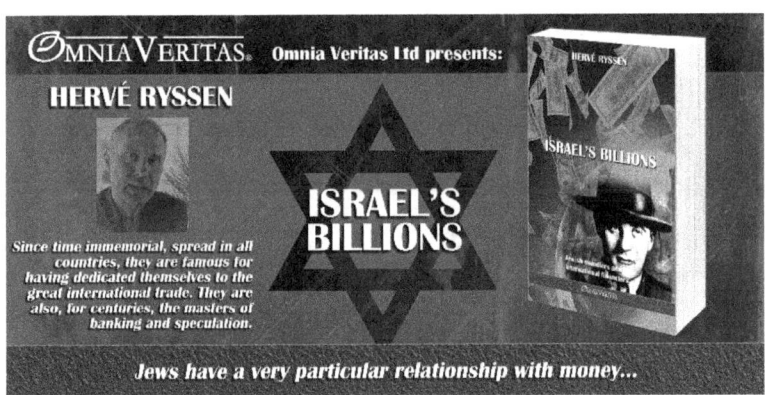

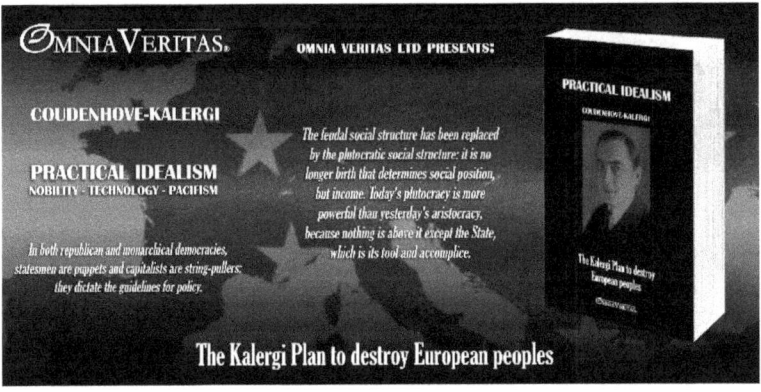

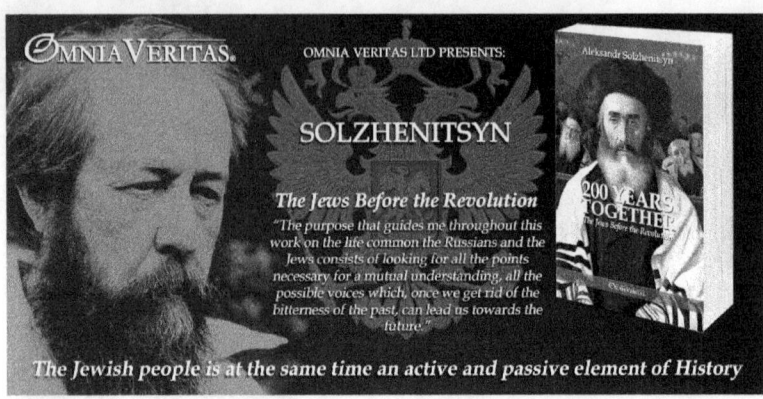

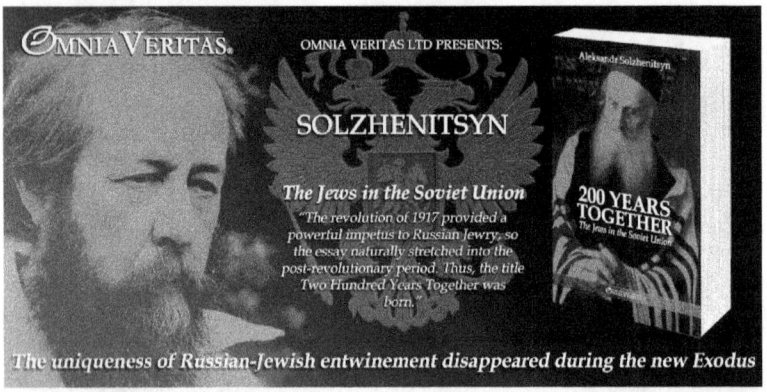

www.ingramcontent.com/pod-product-compliance
Lightning Source LLC
Chambersburg PA
CBHW060817190426
43197CB00038B/1916